THE DOMESTIC CHURCH: ROOM BY ROOM

A Study Guide for Mothers

Donna-Marie Cooper O'Boyle

CIRCLE
PRESS

Cover illustration © Copyright Chaldea Emerson. All rights reserved.
Cover and interior design by Donna Gentile Creative
www.DonnaGentile.com

CIP data is on file with the Library of Congress

ISBN 978-1-933271-20-0

PRINTED IN THE UNITED STATES OF AMERICA

8 7 6 5 4 3 2 1

FIRST EDITION

To all of my children:
Justin, Chaldea, Jessica, Joseph, and Mary-Catherine.
Thank you for all that you are
and all you will be by God's grace.
I forever count my blessings for the gifts of all of you!
I love you always.

Endorsements for *The Domestic Church*

"Donna Marie's latest work is like sharing a spiritual cup of tea with a dear friend. Donna's warm words invite you into the home and guide you step-by-step through the teachings on the domestic church. The pages are filled with direction and guidance from her own years of experience as a mom as well as from the wisdom of the Popes, the saints, and great catechists. Reading this book, pondering the reflections, and applying the thoughtful questions to your own life will be time well spent, and when you're done you will feel refreshed, fulfilled, and comforted, as well as affirmed in your efforts to build a holier family."

Teresa Tomeo, author, speaker,
and syndicated Catholic talk show host

"It was encouraging to read Donna's enthusiastic promotion of ecological breast-feeding, both as a form of natural family planning and for its many health and psychological benefits."

Sheila Kippley, author of Breastfeeding and Catholic Motherhood

"Through her growing body of work, Donna-Marie Cooper O'Boyle has supported and inspired countless mothers. With the publication of *The Domestic Church: Room by Room*, Donna-Marie offers yet another source of enlightenment. This mother's study guide will aid women studying either independently or in intimate groups to grow in their vocations to motherhood. Firmly rooted in Catholic doctrine and complimented by both scriptural and catechetical references, the guide offers a 'room by room' look at the role of spiritual parenting, encompassing every aspect of a woman's life. Small groups will be aided by Donna-Marie's instructions for forming and getting the most out of a small group experience, as well as the helpful Leader's Guide which accompanies the study. I look forward to gathering with a group of my friends to enjoy a study of *The Domestic Church: Room by Room*, and I would highly recommend it to anyone looking to grow in both holiness and familial commitment."

Lisa M. Hendey, founder, CatholicMom.com

"As Catholic mothers, we are supposed to be like the Blessed Mother, saying our 'Yes' to what God asks us every day. Our 'Yes' to him allows love to be born in our homes and in our families. But it is one thing to say yes, and it is quite another to live it! Donna-Marie Cooper O'Boyle has given us an extraordinary gift in this beautiful, lucid, and practical book. As we walk with her from 'room to room,' she helps us to see what it looks like to say 'Yes,' and then she shows us how to live our yes with selflessness, courage, fidelity, and great love. If every parish had a group of mothers who entered deeply into this study, there would be countless moments of 'annunciation' happening all around us, and Love himself could be born in new ways every day, transforming our homes, our families, and our Church."

Sally Robb, wife, mother of six, and radio host of Thread of Grace *and* Mary's Touch *on Catholic Radio International*

"In our houses, too, there are many mansions. Through this series of studies, Donna shows us how every domestic doorway opens to an infinity of glory. We don't need to retreat to a cloister to be contemplatives. God's at home with us, waiting for us to feel at home with him."

Mike Aquilina, executive vice president, St. Paul Center for Biblical Theology, EWTN host, and author of Love in the Little Things

"There are many things that make *The Domestic Church: Room by Room* exceptional, not the least of which is its unique and distinctive approach in presenting a provocative study on the vocation of motherhood. Using the deep and rich Catholic traditions and its Church documents as the foundation, Donna-Marie Cooper O'Boyle succeeds in setting a lovely and inviting table for the reader to come and feast. Just as importantly, she extends a straightforward request to let it be an opportunity to partake in long hours of fellowship.

"I especially liked the familiar, sister-to-sister, intimate tone of each chapter. In a seemingly simple yet thorough manner, prolific author Cooper O'Boyle masterfully weaves Church documents, practical suggestions for couples, spiritual motherhood insights, and candid snapshots from her own marriage and family experience. *The Domestic Church* is an invitation to readers, but in a special way to women, to take time to meditate prayerfully on the holiness present in the quotidian aspects of our day-to-day living.

"But do not mistake *The Domestic Church* for 'just' another book on motherhood. While it is practical and yes, domestic, in its approach, *The Domestic Church* is not only hands-on in its useful topics and discussions, it also gifts the reader with an overview of the all-encompassing richness of the Catholic faith, and it does so with trustworthy accuracy. This is an enlightening, prayerful presentation into the 'sublime privilege and awesome responsibility' that is motherhood. Come and feast!"

María de Lourdes Ruiz Scaperlanda *is an award-winning author and mother of four living in Norman, Oklahoma. Her books include* The Journey: A Guide for the Modern Pilgrim, The Seeker's Guide to Mary, Edith Stein: St. Teresa Benedicta of the Cross, *and T*he Complete Idiot's Guide to Mary of Nazareth. *Maria's Web site is www.mymaria.net.*

TABLE OF CONTENTS

Foreword ix

Preface xi

How to Use This Study Guide xiii

Leader's Guide: Getting Started xv

Chapter One – The Foyer:
Our Blessed Mother Mary and Motherhood. 1

Part One – "I Am the Handmaid of the Lord" 2

Part Two – "To Serve Means to Reign" 12

Chapter Two – The Garage: A Husband in the Picture 29

Part One – Husband and Wife: United in Love 30

Part Two – Differences and Complimentarity 40

Chapter Three – The Nursery: The Blessings of Little Souls 55

*Part One – Open to the Gift of Life: Our "Human
and Christian Responsibility"* 56

Part Two: A Special Communion with the Mystery of Life 76

Chapter Four – The Living Room: In the Heart of the Home 87

Part One – Care of the Hearth: Domestic Happiness 88

Part Two – Everyday Holiness: First and Foremost Educator 100

Chapter Five – The Kitchen: A Vocation of Love 117

Part One – A Love that Compels Us 118

Part Two – A Love that Challenges Us 125

Chapter Six – The Dining Room:
Praying in the Domestic Church. 135

Part One: A Praying Mother – Sanctifying Herself and Her Family. . .136

*Part Two: A Praying Family – Sanctifying the Ecclesial
Community and the World* 144

Chapter Seven – The Basement:
SelflessLove – The Foot of the Cross 155

Part One – "A Living Love Hurts". 156

*Part Two – A Mother's Beatitudes:
Paradoxical Promises that Sustain Our Hope*. 166

Chapter Eight – The Porch: An Overflowing Chalice of Love 177

Part One – Be Kind and Merciful. 178

*Part Two – The Face of Christ:
Finding God in Each Brother and Sister*. .191

Chapter Nine – The Patio:
Evangelizing with the Feminine Genius .199

Part One – To the Ends of the Earth! 200

Part Two – Called to be a Luminous Sign of the Presence of Christ. . .210

Leader's Guide: Answers 227

Acknowledgements. 251

About the Author 253

FOREWORD

When Donna first asked me to write the Foreword to this book, I was not only honored but intrigued as well. I love the term "domestic church" and agree wholeheartedly that our families and our homes must be places where God remains always at the center, places where we lay down a foundation of faith and build up Gospel-centered lives. And yet it can be hard to know how to turn that beautiful, poetic sentiment into practical, tangible reality. With this book, Donna takes us through each "room" of our lives, guiding us deeper into the mystery of faith that exists in every corner of our domestic church and then sharing with us the tools and insights needed to coax that mystery out into the light of day where it can blossom into the kind of transforming love that we are called to be to one another.

The Domestic Church: Room by Room is so much more than a "Mother's Study Guide" for women who want to deepen their understanding of their vocations. It is an exploration of Catholic teaching as it relates to our roles as women, wives, mothers, and citizens of the world at large. Referring back to Scripture, papal encyclicals, apostolic letters, the Catechism of the Catholic Church, and the words of the great saints, Donna weaves together the life story of every Catholic woman, regardless of her age, background, family situation, or career choice. Through stories from her own life, including the personal friendship she shared with Blessed Mother Teresa of Calcutta, Donna demystifies the domestic church, offering concrete ways to find joy and spiritual fulfillment in the "nitty-gritty, humble work" of our daily lives.

In Donna's hands, the busyness of life that threatens to leave us worn out both physically and spiritually becomes one more opportunity to find God in the details. Suddenly, retreating into the silence of our hearts amid the chaos of our lives seems attainable, and that's no small feat. Of course, it doesn't surprise me that Donna can inspire such lofty goals. As I've gotten to know Donna, I've learned that she is the kind of person who inspires everyone she meets – and even those she doesn't. Donna and I have never met in person, and yet, through her warmth and generosity of spirit and deep faith, we have forged a friendship. Our shared paths as writers and mothers and seekers of the Truth have drawn us together, even if only by email and phone. I feel blessed to know her.

Now I feel doubly blessed to have some small role in her endeavor to help women find the deep well of holiness that exists in their day-to-day lives. When I began reading *The Domestic Church*, I was feeling stressed by the household chores that were piling up, by the work deadlines that were looming, by the bickering between my children that never seems to end. By the time I finished, I felt at peace, knowing that while the chores and the deadlines and the bickering may still be there, I can take heart in the greater purpose that exists in the "nitty-gritty." I have no doubt you will find the same sense of peace and spiritual satisfaction in the pages that follow.

Mary DeTurris Poust, author of The Complete Idiot's Guide to the Catholic Catechism *and* Parenting a Grieving Child, *contributing editor for* Our Sunday Visitor, *and award-winning "Life Lines" columnist*

Preface

The gift of conceiving and carrying a human life within one's own body – under one's heart – and then giving birth to and raising this little person is almost beyond depiction – and nothing short of miraculous. The gift of a child entrusted to a woman through adoption is also an incredible blessing.

The vocation of motherhood is a sublime privilege and an awesome responsibility. By partaking in a partnership with God, through her marital vows, a mother experiences a special communion with the mystery of life as it develops within her very being. In the case of adoption, a mother also experiences motherly bonding and communion with the new life that has been entrusted to her. Pope John Paul II has told us that this communion "is decisive in laying the foundation for a new human personality" as she raises her child. Mothers are also remarkably responsible to some degree for the sanctification of their spouses and their children.

I wish to impress upon mothers what a *gift* it is to be a mother. Our vocation is filled to the brim with blessings, abounding with joy, beauty, and grace when we wholeheartedly embrace it with prayerful hearts! "The Christian home is the place where children receive the first proclamation of the faith. For this reason the family home is rightly called 'the domestic church,' a community of grace and prayer, a school of human virtues and of Christian charity," we learn from the Catechism (CCC, 1666). Pope Benedict XVI tells us, "Every home is called to become a 'domestic church' in which family life is completely centered on the lordship of Christ and the love of husband and wife mirrors the mystery of Christ's love for the Church, his Bride." Our Lord has gifted us with the blessing of a family in which we live in communion with one another during our day-to-day activities, where we center our lives on the lordship of Christ, and where we actually work out our salvation together inside and outside the walls of our domestic church!

In this grace-filled year of 2008, which is the twentieth anniversary of *Mulieris Dignitatem* (On the Dignity and Vocation of Women) and the fortieth anniversary of *Humanae Vitae* (On Human Life), I am honored and privileged to bring you this study on the vocation of motherhood. May God bless you and your families in great abundance!

"Yes indeed, the families of today must be called back to their original position. They must follow Christ."
– Pope John Paul II, *Familiaris Consortio*
(The Role of the Christian Family in the Modern World)

How to Use This Study Guide

You may have picked up this book because you are a mother seeking deeper holiness and understanding of your vocation. Or perhaps you are a mother-to-be, wanting to prepare your heart for the birth of your first child and everything that entails, or you are an engaged woman about to be married and would like to be prepared for your future wedded life. Whatever the case may be, this book can be a wonderful retreat. Pause with Our Lord and his Blessed Mother as you explore topics, questions, situations, and Church teaching; search your heart as you grow in holiness!

This study guide focuses on the vocation of motherhood. It may be carried out independently by reading through and reflecting upon each lesson alone and answering the questions. You may then refer to the Leader's Guide in the back of the book to compare your answers. Ideally, this mother's study guide works very well for a group of mothers, mothers-to-be, and engaged women. In this way, you will benefit by the sharing, camaraderie, and insights of other like-minded women, enabling you to learn more about your faith in God and the teachings of the Catholic Church – not to mention having a little fun in the process, too!

You may want to refer to the excerpts and readings within this book for encouragement and direction at various times throughout your mothering journey, since we all grow in holiness with time. Reviewing and studying this again will inspire you, in different ways, to even greater virtue. You may also wish to invite a different group of women to participate in this study at another time.

The Leader's Guide (with answers) included in this book will assist you in conducting this mother's study for a group. Bear in mind that there will be personal answers, as most of the questions presented will solicit reflection on one's own life. The next section, Leader's Guide: Getting Started, will provide some ideas for getting your mother's study underway.

I have quoted a number of Church documents throughout this study. I encourage you to become more familiar with these documents by reading them and reflecting upon the wealth of knowledge, insight, and inspiration they contain. You may easily access them online through the Vatican Web site (http://www.vatican.va) or purchase copies at a Catholic bookstore.

To give this mother's study a cozier feel, I have broken up the topics of discussion into *rooms* in your domestic church. A Bible, a copy of the Catechism of the Catholic Church (referred to in this study as Catechism or CCC), and an open and prayerful heart are all that is required to participate in this mother's study. Retreat from the ordinary to discover the extraordinary in your vocation of love!

> *"Each and every time that motherhood is repeated in human history, it is always related to the Covenant which God established with the human race through the motherhood of the Mother of God."*
> – Pope John Paul II, *Mulieris Dignitatem*

Leader's Guide: Getting Started

It's wonderful that you have decided to take on the task of leading this mother's study! You have no doubt been inspired to do so, and Our Lord will certainly reward your efforts. Find some time to prayerfully prepare before each session. A visit to the Blessed Sacrament would be ideal. However, quiet prayer within your "domestic church" is just fine. Here are a few general suggestions to help you organize your study. These are not strict or rigid rules – merely suggestions to help things run smoothly. You may, of course, adjust them to your own liking and the needs of the group.

To get started, ask some of your friends and acquaintances from your parish, neighbors, and relatives if they'd like to join you in this motherhood study. Put the whole endeavor in God's hands, asking him to inspire you as to whom you should ask. Someone you may not have thought would be open to this idea may welcome it with great joy! Consider putting an announcement in your parish bulletin to solicit interest. This study is designed for group discussion, so a small membership is preferable. A group of five to eight is ideal, but more or less is fine. Decide upon a set place and time, preferably once a week. You may decide to meet in your home or seek out another location, such as the parish hall. The cozier and more comfortable the setting is the better, so that all feel welcome and relaxed enough to learn and share. Remember to look at the calendar and be mindful of holidays, school closings, or holy days that may fall during your sessions and adjust your schedule accordingly. Make a list of the pertinent information to give each member at the first session or beforehand.

1. It is recommended that you cover one chapter per week. Your time together should be between one and two hours. You can ask the members what they would prefer since their time away from home is usually a luxury, and some participants will most likely be mothers with small children that require babysitting. You may find that some chapters may take two sessions to cover properly, but it's up to you and your group.

2. The atmosphere should always be friendly and welcoming. Everyone should feel comfortable to speak and share at the appropriate times. Refreshments are a nice addition. Oftentimes, lively and inspiring discussions occur around the coffee cake afterwards! You can provide the refreshments at the first session, then make a sign-up sheet and ask for volunteers to provide refreshments for each additional session.

3. Begin and end each session with a prayer. You may want to ask each member to voice a prayer petition after your main prayer or prayers. You may also, after the ending prayer, ask that each member pray daily for each other and for God's holy will for the group. You will then be united in prayer throughout the week.

4. As leader of the group, you will need to prepare before each session. Take some time to sit down with the selected lesson and pray. Prepare any additional information that you wish to discuss that will tie in to the study, being careful, of course, to use only materials that are approved by the magisterium of the Church. Always have your Bible (I have used the *New Revised Standard Version, Catholic Edition* in my quotes throughout), a copy of the Catechism of the Catholic Church, and a copy of this study guide at each session.

5. During the session, your job is to facilitate by first leading the prayers and then by going through the chapter, perhaps getting volunteers to read sections. Next, you will go through the questions, encouraging input and sharing. You may want to remind the members that some of their answers may be very personal; they may prefer to keep those answers private. You will be in charge of keeping the discussion moving and correcting any misunderstandings so that errors about the Catholic faith are not taught inadvertently. If

there is something that you are not certain about, tell the members that you are going to check with your priest or spiritual advisor and get back to them on that subject the following week. This way there will never be worry on your part if you feel that you can't address something as appropriately or as detailed as you'd like.

6. Ask each member to complete the assigned chapter before each meeting. To extend the theme of each session a bit and to keep it all enveloped in prayer, you may want to photocopy or write down the prayer for the upcoming session in advance. This prayer is located at the end of each chapter. You can be as creative as you like with this. It's not necessary to be an artist! Simply print the prayer out on fancy paper, adding religious or feminine stickers, or paste the prayer onto little file cards that the members can decorate themselves and then slip into their Bible or prayer book. Give these prayers to the members and ask them to pray the prayer each day throughout the week leading up to your next meeting. Give the members the first prayer when they register for this retreat.

May God bless your mother's study!
Through him, it will be grace-filled and fulfilling!

1. The Foyer:
Our Blessed Mother Mary and Motherhood

"And Mary said,

'Behold, I am the

handmaid of the

Lord; let it be to me

according to your word.'

And the angel

departed from her."

~ Lk 1:38

PART ONE 🌿 "I AM THE HANDMAID OF THE LORD"

Read Luke 1:26-56. When thinking of Mary, the Mother of God and her own motherhood of Jesus, we may not feel naturally inclined to relate or compare our own motherhood to hers. Perhaps it may seem utterly impossible. Mary, after all, was without sin. She was given God's tremendous gift of carrying the Redeemer of the world in her own womb, then giving birth to him and raising him with St. Joseph.

Many factors may cause us to conclude that Mary is in reality too far removed from our lives for us to be able to relate to her motherhood. After all, in addition to her holiness, her Jewish feet walked on this earth so long ago in a far-off place. Nevertheless, do we dare ask ourselves: "How can a simple mother like me aspire to imitate such an amazing Mother? And in so imitating Mother Mary, will I glorify and please God?"

We can ponder Mary's life a bit and recall the momentous occasion when the Angel Gabriel visited the teenaged Mary, announcing to her that she would become the Mother of God (Lk 1:26-39). Being very humble, Mary may have found it difficult to believe that a simple girl like her would be chosen by God. Scripture tells us that Mary "went in haste to a Judean town in the hill country" (Lk 1:39). When Mary took that blessing immediately to her heart, she responded with a courageous "Yes" to God.

Shortly afterward, Mary's determination and generous heart sent her – alone, on foot, and pregnant – on a three-day journey to help her cousin Elizabeth, who was much older and also expecting a child. We can be sure that Mary prayed and reflected all throughout her journey because the blessedness of Jesus dwelled within the tabernacle of her womb.

Perhaps I can imagine Our Lord asking me for my "Yes." Is he asking for my "Yes" in surrender to his will for me? I may want to consider that Mary's "Yes" to God was not a mediocre, "Okay, I guess so." Rather, she wholeheartedly embraced God's holy will for her life and all that entailed. I should consider all of my responses to God as a mother, reflecting upon my willingness – or lack thereof – to accept everything that God has for me. Am I willing to accept God's holy will with joy? This is not necessarily always an easy task as a mother.

Mary's determination and generous heart sent her - alone, on foot, and pregnant - on a three-day journey to help her cousin Elizabeth, who was much older and also expecting a child. We can be sure that Mary prayed and reflected all throughout her journey because the blessedness of Jesus dwelled within the tabernacle of her womb.

In these first few reflections recalling and pondering Mary's life, we can call to mind some of the virtues that Mary demonstrated in her response to God. We see that she was steadfast in faith and trust, even though it probably seemed outrageous to her that she was being called to be the Mother of God. Nevertheless, again we recognize that Mary was courageous with her answer, wanting only what God wanted of her. She was also generous with the gifts that God had given her; she didn't dwell on her own pregnancy, but rather, went in "haste," giving selflessly to help her pregnant and elderly cousin Elizabeth. We can also pray for courage in our own vocation of motherhood, as well as for a Mary-like sensitive attentiveness to the care and needs of others.

It is necessary for us to remember that Mary was truly human like us, just living in a different era as a faithful and prayerful Jewish woman. Therefore, she possessed her own free will. She could easily have said "No" to God out of fear or selfishness. Because she was human she needed to be steadfast in faith to be able to courageously answer God with her fiat. She illustrated that she was faithful to prayer as well as quiet enough within her own heart to listen to God calling her.

We learn from *Redemptoris Mater* (Mother of the Redeemer), "Indeed, at the Annunciation Mary entrusted herself to God completely, with the 'full submission of intellect and will,' manifesting 'the obedience of faith' to him who spoke to her through his messenger. She responded, therefore, with all her human and feminine 'I' and this response of faith included both perfect cooperation with 'the grace of God that precedes and assists' and perfect openness to the action of the Holy Spirit, who 'constantly brings faith to completion by his gifts.'"

A mother can learn from Mary by asking for God's grace to entrust herself completely to him with the "full submission of intellect and will."

Love that Suffers

We also know that our Blessed Mother lived a life of suffering along with her Son Jesus. When she and Joseph brought Jesus to the Temple forty days after his birth, Simeon told Mary that a sword of sorrow would pierce her heart. Mary truly lived her Son's pain as she partook in every aspect of his life and suffering – from witnessing the scorn of some of the people towards Jesus and his teachings, watching him get scourged and beaten on the road to Calvary, following him to the foot of the Cross, and then holding his lifeless body in her arms.

She is a mother who understands pain and suffering. We shouldn't be afraid to call upon her because she knows all about a mother's love and the suffering and pain that are required of us.

As Mary stood at the foot of the Cross, she knew that it was her Son's death that would bring life to the world. Even so, her heart was breaking. "Here is your Mother," Jesus said from the Cross (Jn 19:26-27). He entrusted Mary to John and John to Mary. The disciple John actually represented the whole Christian community, so Mary became the Mother of the whole Church at her Son's request. She became the new Eve (Jn 19:26). Her call in life was being constantly fulfilled because she had given herself completely to the will of the Father.

As Pope John Paul II reminds us, "The words uttered by Jesus from the Cross signify that the motherhood of her who bore Christ finds a 'new' continuation in the Church and through the Church, symbolized and represented by John. In this way, she who as the one 'full of grace' was brought into the mystery of Christ in order to be his Mother and thus the Holy Mother of God, through the Church remains in that mystery as 'the woman' spoken of by the Book of Genesis (3:15) at the beginning and by the Apocalypse (12:1) at the end of the history of salvation. In accordance with the eternal plan of Providence, Mary's divine motherhood is to be poured out upon the Church, as indicated by statements of Tradition, according to which Mary's 'motherhood' of the Church is the reflection and extension of her motherhood of the Son of God" (*Redemptoris Mater*, 1987).

Another form of suffering that our Blessed Mother Mary experienced was a great deal of concern and heartache when her Son was missing for three days as a twelve-year-old child. Mary was grateful when she found him; her heavy heart was relieved: "Child, why have you treated us like this? Look, your father and I have been searching for you in great anxiety" (Lk 2:48). But Mary immediately accepted her Son's mission as Jesus explained it to her. Modern day mothers endure similar heartache, concern, and suffering, and Our Blessed Mother can help us when we call upon her when we are going through challenging situations with our families.

The Holy Spirit that overshadowed Mary at the Annunciation again came to her at Pentecost (Acts 1:14) where she received guidance for herself and the Church. We can be sure that the Holy Spirit was always active in our Blessed Mother Mary's life. A mother can also ask the Holy Spirit to be active and alive throughout her vocation as well.

"Mary was, from that instant on, the only one who was able to confirm with complete sincerity, This is my body. She offered her body, her strength, her whole being, to form the body of Christ."

Blessed Teresa of Calcutta described our Blessed Mother's generous heart eloquently when she said, "I believe that our mother the Church has elevated women to a great honor in the presence of God by proclaiming Mary the Mother of the Church. God so loved the world that he gave his Son. This was the first Eucharist: the gift of his Son, when he gave him to Our Lady, establishing in her the first altar.

"Mary was, from that instant on, the only one who was able to confirm with complete sincerity, *This is my body.* She offered her body, her strength, her whole being, to form the body of Christ.

"It was on her that power of the Holy Spirit rested and in her that the Word became flesh. Mary gave herself to him completely because she had previously consecrated herself to him – in order to preserve her virginity virgin, her purity pure, and her chastity chaste, and in order to offer them to the only living God.

"When the angel announced to Mary the coming of Christ, she only posed a question: she could not understand how she could take back the gift of herself that she had made to God. The angel explained it, and she understood immediately. Her lips uttered a beautiful response that asserted all that she was as a woman: 'I am the servant of the Lord. Let it be done to me as you say'" (Blessed Teresa of Calcutta, in a talk given at the Forty-First International Eucharistic Congress in Philadelphia, August 7, 1976).

We know that we will never accomplish what our Blessed Mother has, or be able to come close to her holiness, yet we are also called to holiness in the sublime role of raising our children. Our Mother Mary gives us so many attributes and virtues to emulate in our vocation as a mother. We can look to Mary and realize that her deep faith was really the foundation of her holiness. We can remember that Mary was human like us and needed to pray so that she would be unwavering in her faith, just as we mothers are called to do. Mary's faith is the same gift that is available to us. We can ask Our Lord for the gift of an increasing faith and ask Mary to be a mother to us, guiding us closer to her Son Jesus. Let's allow our Blessed Mother to enter through the foyers of our homes and our hearts. In doing so, we will be allowing her to inspire us to a deeper faith and we will also be welcoming Our Lord and his holy will for our lives. What better way to get closer to Our Lord than through his mother?

1. How did Mary's "Yes" to life and to God affect my life?

_____

_____

_____

_____

_____

_____

_____

_____

2. What are three practical ways in which I can imitate our Blessed Mother's virtues discussed thus far?

_____

_____

_____

_____

_____

_____

_____

_____

_____

3. *Where might God be calling me to answer him with my own courageous "Yes!"?*

_____

_____

_____

_____

_____

_____

_____

4. *How can I be quiet in my soul so I can hear what God is telling me?*

_____

_____

_____

_____

_____

_____

_____

Part Two ꩜ "To Serve Means to Reign"

Pope John Paul II told us in *Redemtoris Mater*, "She who at the Annunciation called herself the 'handmaid of the Lord' remained throughout her earthly life faithful to what this name expresses. In this she confirmed that she was a true 'disciple' of Christ, who strongly emphasized that his mission was one of service: the Son of man 'came not to be served but to serve, and to give his life as a ransom for many' (Mt 20:28). In this way, Mary became the first of those who, 'serving Christ also in others, with humility and patience lead her brothers and sisters to that King whom to serve is to reign,' and she fully obtained that 'state of royal freedom' proper to Christ's disciples: to serve means to reign!"

What do Pope John Paul's words mean to me in this regard? I can reflect on how our Blessed Mother lived her life as a "handmaid of the Lord," wanting nothing more than to serve and remain humble. Yet, because of God's grace, Mary would take her place within Christ's messianic mission of service. Jesus has clearly shown and lived the royal dignity in service and often spoke about it. He said, "The Son of Man came not to be served but to serve" (Mk 10:45). Isaiah's prophesy points to Christ's awareness of his messianic mission and role as the Redeemer of the World. We are reminded again in the Gospel of Matthew: "Just as the son of man came not to be served but to serve, and to give his life a ransom for many" (Mt 20:28).

In *Mulieris Dignitatem* Pope John Paul II tells us, "It is precisely this service which constitutes the very foundation of that Kingdom in which 'to serve...means to reign.'" This royal dignity of service is joined to the vocation of every person. We can pause and reflect a few moments upon this paradoxical royalty intertwined with service. In my sublime role as a mother to a family, am I not also given a dignified and significant position in the heart of the home, and at the same time, am I not also called to *serve* my family?

Pope Benedict XVI also reminds us about Mary's gift of self in service to others: "Overcoming death [she] told us: 'Courage, love wins in the end! My life means that I am God's handmaid; my life means giving myself to God and my fellow man as a gift'" (August 15th, 2007).

Speaking of Mary's dignity and vocation, Pope John Paul II notes, "In anything we think, say, or do concerning the dignity and the vocation of women, our thoughts, hearts, and actions must not become detached from this horizon. The dignity of every human being and vocation corresponding to that dignity find their definitive measure in *union with God*. Mary, the woman of the Bible, is the most complete expression of this dignity and vocation. For no human being, male or female, created in the image and likeness of God, can *in any way* attain fulfillment apart from this image and likeness" *(Mulieris Dignitatem,* II, 5).

"All Generations Will Call Me Blessed"

The Catechism tells us, "'The Church's devotion to the Blessed Virgin is intrinsic to Christian worship.' The Church rightly honors the Blessed Virgin with special devotion. From the most ancient times the Blessed Virgin has been honored with the title of 'Mother of God,' to whose protection the faithful fly in all their dangers and needs…. This very special devotion…differs essentially from the adoration which is given to the incarnate Word and equally to the Father and the Holy Spirit, and greatly fosters this adoration. The liturgical feasts dedicated to the Mother of God and Marian prayer, such as the rosary, an 'epitome of the whole Gospel,' express this devotion to the Virgin Mary" (CCC, 971).

A Catholic mother is gifted with the richness of her Catholic Church down through the ages, as well as with the model of our

Blessed Mother who guides her to be of service to others – a message we find reiterated through our Holy Fathers and the saints. Our Lord Jesus himself urges us on to imitate him and his Mother in service to our fellow man: "A new commandment I give to you, that you love one another; even as I have loved you, that you also love one another" (Jn 13:34).

For mothers, this means service first in her family and then reaching out to the world. At times, good intentions and a mother's loving heart may cause her to stretch herself too much to administer to the needs of others outside her home. It's wonderful and holy to want to help, yet mothers must remember that their love begins first and foremost at home. When a mother is certain that her family's needs are satisfied in the home, she can then consider ways in which she would like to help others in the community. Being sure that her family is properly cared for before she embarks in other areas of ministry or gets involved in too many committees will ensure that she is not inadvertently neglecting her family in the process of helping others.

Reflecting on this Gospel message of loving one another, Blessed Teresa of Calcutta admonished us: "These words should not only be a light to us, but also a flame consuming the selfishness which prevents the growth of holiness. Jesus loved us to the end, to the very limit of love, the Cross. Love must come from within – from our union with Christ – an outpouring of our love for God. Loving should be as normal to us as living and breathing, day after day until our deaths." These beautiful words come from a holy woman who wanted to die on her feet while caring for the poorest of the poor.

A mother's love should be selfless and will indeed grow deeper as she continues to grow in holiness. Calling upon Our Lord and his Blessed Mother for an increase in grace, strength, faith, hope, and love often each day, her union with Christ will become obvious to those around her as she loves with Christ's love; this will undoubtedly draw others to Christ.

The role of motherhood is a blessing to both mother and family because the very act of mothering becomes a "flame" that consumes the selfishness that Blessed Teresa spoke of. Would a mother leave her baby to cry in pain to run after some other pursuit? Would a faithful mother neglect her family willfully to satisfy any selfish desire? She simply cannot. The vocation of motherhood draws a mother out of herself and into a role of service and extreme love – a love that cannot be fully understood except by God or a mother, a love that will sacrifice itself for the other even to the point of death. Certainly, fathers too, are drawn to a role of service and selfless and sacrificial love. But mothers most times feel this responsibility to their offspring through an innate, hands-on way by virtue of their vocation.

Our Blessed Mother teaches us the value and holiness in obedience to the Father's will through faith, hope, and love. In *Lumen Gentium* (On the Church) we read, "By her complete adherence to the Father's will, to his Son's redemptive work, and to every prompting of the Holy Spirit, the Virgin Mary is the Church's model of faith and charity. Thus she is a 'preeminent and…wholly unique member of the Church; indeed, she is the 'exemplary realization' (typus) of the Church.

"Her role in relation to the Church and to all humanity goes still further. 'In a wholly singular way she cooperated by her obedience, faith, hope, and burning charity in the Savior's work of restoring supernatural life to souls. For this reason she is a mother to us in the order of grace.'

By her complete adherence to the Father's will, to his Son's redemptive work, and to every prompting of the Holy Spirit, the Virgin Mary is the Church's model of faith and charity.

"This motherhood of Mary in the order of grace continues uninterruptedly from the consent which she loyally gave at the Annunciation and which she sustained without wavering beneath the Cross, until the eternal fulfillment of all the elect. Taken up to heaven she did not lay aside this saving office but by her manifold intercession continues to bring us the gifts of eternal salvation... Therefore the Blessed Virgin is invoked in the Church under the titles of Advocate, Helper, Benefactor, and Mediatrix'" (LG, 61-62).

Under the many titles that Mary personifies, she is without a doubt a powerful intercessor for mothers. She wants to mother us and protect our families. We mothers need only ask for her intercession.

Our Blessed Mother has much to teach mothers. We can certainly pray for the grace to learn from Mary and emulate her virtues. Blessed Teresa who had a special relationship with Mary has told us, "Mary can teach us silence – how to keep all things in our hearts as she did, to pray in the silence of our hearts.

"Mary can teach us kindness – she went in haste to serve Elizabeth. 'They have no wine,' she told Jesus at Cana. Let us, like her, be aware of the needs of the poor, be they spiritual or material and let us, like her, give generously of the love and grace we are granted.

"Mary will teach us humility – though full of grace yet only the handmaid of the Lord, she stands as one of us at the foot of the Cross, a sinner needing redemption. Let us, like her, touch the dying, the poor, the lonely, and the unwanted according to the graces we have received, and let us not be ashamed or slow to do the humble work" (Mother Teresa's Lessons of Love).

Mothers may feel, or even be convinced, that it impossible to find silence in a busy (and sometimes) very noisy household. Blessed Teresa assures us that the Blessed Mother can teach us how to find it. Silence can ironically be found in the busyness of a mother's day as a mother learns to retreat to her heart even as she is involved in the care of her family. Within the "silence" of a mother's heart, Our Lord can speak.

At times, the hectic pace and the constant and immediate demands placed on her can cause a mother to feel inadequate or lacking direction in her spiritual life, simply because she feels she has no time to pray. It is when she realizes that Our Lord actually wants to use her attentiveness to her family's needs that she will understand the value and prayerfulness in performing little things with great love. The mother becomes an everyday example to her family as she raises her children in holiness and goes about with a prayerful heart, striving to emulate the Blessed Mother's virtues.

But she's not wearing a halo yet! Naturally, she will feel annoyed or upset at the sometimes chaotic tone in the household or bouts of sibling rivalry. Yet, she is there to help calm it down, keep the peace, and steer everyone in the right direction. A family is a true "work in progress"! All the while, a mother can be mindful of following Blessed Teresa's advice to "not be ashamed of the humble work" which is a huge part of mothering: an extraordinary vocation in which little saints are raised inside the hidden confines of homelife amid the nitty-gritty, humble work of the mother in the home.

1. How can I acquire freedom in my heart, based on the material I just read in Part Two?

_____

_____

_____

_____

_____

_____

_____

_____

2. How is the "royal dignity of service" that Pope John Paul II spoke about joined to the vocation of every person and specifically my vocation of motherhood? How do I become more like Jesus and Mary when I serve? Read Mk 10:45 and Mt 20:28.

_____

_____

_____

_____

_____

_____

_____

3. Read Jn 13:12-17. In what ways can I give myself as a gift?

_____

_____

_____

_____

_____

_____

_____

_____

_____

4. Where does love truly come from?

_____

_____

_____

_____

_____

_____

_____

_____

5. Just as the virtues are apparent in Mary's life, how can the virtues of faith, hope, and love be shown in my life?

_____

_____

_____

_____

_____

_____

_____

Summing Up

We have been discussing how our Blessed Mother Mary can help us in our own mothering by being a model for us and also by her intercession. We have looked a bit at her virtuous life and her heroic practice of the virtues.

We can see that the driving force behind all of the virtues is *love*. The Catechism tells us that "charity is the theological virtue by which we love God above all things for his own sake, and our neighbor as ourselves for the love of God.

"Jesus makes charity the *new commandment*. By loving his own 'to the end,' he makes manifest the Father's love which he receives. By loving one another, the disciples imitate the love of Jesus which they themselves receive. Whence Jesus says: 'As the Father has loved me, so I have loved you; abide in my love.' And again: 'This is my commandment, that you love one another as I have loved you'" (CCC, 1822-1822). If we do not possess Christ's love in our own hearts, we will fall drastically short in loving and serving our families properly.

Blessed Mother Teresa reminds us, "Love must come from within – from our union with Christ – an outpouring of our love for God. Loving should be as normal to us as living and breathing, day after day until our deaths."

We are all called to union with God. Pope John Paul II told us that "the dignity of every human being and vocation corresponding to that dignity find their definitive measure in *union with God*." He emphasized that Mary is "the most complete expression of this dignity and vocation."

We have learned that "to serve means to reign." Jesus himself served, his Blessed Mother served, and we are also called to serve in so many ways within our families by giving of ourselves to bring forth life and then caring for the lives that Our Lord has entrusted to us.

Thoughts to Ponder

If Mary, who was the Mother of God, can be his handmaid, taking delight in serving others, I can certainly strive to be a handmaid, too. Within my vocation of motherhood I will find a deep and lasting peace when I become intimately united to Christ while striving to be a servant to others, especially within my own family. Through the gift of myself, I receive so much in return – much more than I can ever imagine.

A life of prayer is necessary to come closer to Jesus and to understand God's holy will for my life. Prayer and the many graces that are bestowed upon me in my vocation will ultimately give me the necessary strength to carry out my duties within my household, as well as to increase the love for my family.

It would be a lie to convey that a mother's daily life is only one of blissful loving embraces and constant "warm fuzzies." Motherhood is intrinsically beautiful, but while she is in the "trenches" with whiny demands, diapers, overflowing hampers of dirty laundry, and the constantly refilling kitchen sink, a mother knows that the feeling of love for her family may not always emerge easily in every circumstance. It will, at times, come through the sacrifice of giving of herself and her decision to remain faithful to her vocation. A mother *decides* to love and to continue to love her family in God's plan for her salvation and the salvation of her family. Through a mother's loving service, God is at work sanctifying her soul when she thoroughly surrenders her heart to his holy will.

When life seems difficult within the family, I have recourse to the Blessed Mother who was human like me and will truly understand my problems. She will intercede for me; she is waiting to hear my prayers. Mothers can learn from Mary who is an example of one who listened to God and allowed the Holy Spirit to inspire and guide her. I can learn from Mary that a mother's prayer is powerful. When I am asked to endure suffering or pain within my role as a mother, I can turn my thoughts to Mother Mary and ask her assistance and intercession. Throughout difficulties, and while trusting in God during particular situations within my homelife, I can meditate on Mary's faithful trust in Our Lord and in the guidance of the Holy Spirit. When I experience the deep joy in my role as a mother, I can feel an affinity with Mary, who experienced deep joy in mothering Jesus.

Blessed Teresa of Calcutta taught me to say a very simple but poignant prayer to the Blessed Mother. She said, "Mary, Mother of Jesus, be a Mother to me now." Let us invoke her often.

Let us also pray along with Blessed Teresa of Calcutta that the words in John's Gospel to "love one another; even as I have loved you" will "not only be a light to us, but also a flame consuming the selfishness which prevents the growth of holiness" – so that love will permeate our vocation of motherhood.

"Holy Mary, Mother of God, our Mother, teach us to believe, to hope, to love with you. Show us the way to his Kingdom! Star of the Sea, shine upon us and guide us on our way!"

– Benedict XVI, Spe Salvi

PRAYER
please open my heart...

Dear Blessed Mother Mary,

Please open my heart to see the holiness within my vocation of motherhood. Please guide me each day as I guide my children towards heaven. Help me to have the courage to strive to serve others as you did, rather than expect to be served. I pray that I may also be a "handmaid of the Lord." I pray for the courage to say to the Lord, "Be it done unto me according to thy Word."
Teach me, please, dear holy Mary, and bring me to your Son Jesus.

Amen.

2. The Garage:
A Husband in the Picture

"Husbands,

love your wives,

just as Christ loved

the Church

and gave himself

up for her."

~ Eph 5:25

Part One ❧ Husband and Wife: United in Love

I love how Pope Benedict began his first encyclical, *Deus Caritas Est* (God Is Love). First, he quoted the beautiful verse from the First Letter of John about love: "God is love, and he who abides in love abides in God, and God abides in him." Then he explained the different kinds of love and continued, "Amid this multiplicity of meanings, however, one in particular stands out: love between man and woman, where body and soul are inseparably joined and human beings glimpse an apparently irresistible promise of happiness. This would seem to be the epitome of love; all other kinds of love immediately seem to fade in comparison." What beautiful words for a husband and wife to ponder!

You and your husband undoubtedly grew together in love throughout your courting days. You married because you were attracted to one another in many ways, for a variety of reasons, and knew that the love that you shared was a blessing that was meant to be eternal. The two of you became *one* when you proclaimed your "I do" to one another at the altar. Since your wedding day, you have been growing together throughout the reality of your daily lives – through thick and thin. By God's grace, you have actually become of "God's love for humanity and the love of Christ the

Church his bride" (*Familiaris Consortio*, 17).

given a Christian couple an identity and a mission.

aul II profoundly proclaimed that, "Each family finds

a summons that cannot be ignored, and that specifies

ty and its responsibility: Family, *become* what you *are*."

naturally begin with husband and wife. God gives us

usband to work together and to *become* what we are

ind in the discovering of our identity and mission, we

r Lord.

el of Matthew we read, "For this reason, a man shall

and mother and be joined to his wife, and the two shall

h" (Mt 19:5-6). We are supposed to *leave* and *cleave* so

me *one*. We make our own new family. When speaking

principle and power of communion," Pope John Paul

liaris Consortio that, "The first communion is the one

ed and which develops between husband and wife:

venant of married life, the man and woman 'are no

e flesh' and they are called to grow continually in

through day-to-day fidelity to their marriage promise

-giving" (*Familiaris Consortio*, 19).

Family, become what you are.

Pope John Paul II's words remind us that husband and wife have made a *covenant* with one another, committing to fidelity each and every day, as well as a promise to give oneself totally to the spouse. Through our self-giving, our marriage blossoms and grows in holiness and maturity. It is through our daily activities and communion with each other that our commitment deepens, especially through the challenges that at times beset us.

The Catechism again reminds us, "Holy Scripture affirms that man and woman were created for one another: 'It is not good that the man should be alone.' The woman, 'flesh of his flesh,' i.e., his counterpart, his equal, his nearest in all things, is given to him by God as a 'helpmate'; she thus represents God from whom comes our help. 'Therefore a man leaves his father and his mother and cleaves to his wife, and they become one flesh.' The Lord himself shows that this signifies an unbreakable union of their two lives by recalling what the plan of the Creator has been 'in the beginning': 'So they are no longer two, but one flesh'" (CCC, 1605).

The sacrament of their marriage unites the couple in love, responsibility, sacrifice, and service to one another. Sometimes this union of hearts in all things may sound "easier said than done," if you know what I mean. However, a love that is authentic, devoted, a reflection of "God's love for humanity and the love of Christ the Lord for the Church his bride" (*Familiaris Consortio*, 17).

God has given a Christian couple an identity and a mission. Pope John Paul II profoundly proclaimed that, "Each family finds within itself a summons that cannot be ignored, and that specifies both its dignity and its responsibility: Family, *become* what you *are*." Our families naturally begin with husband and wife. God gives us the gift of a husband to work together and to *become* what we are meant to be, and in the discovering of our identity and mission, we will glorify Our Lord.

In the Gospel of Matthew we read, "For this reason, a man shall leave his father and mother and be joined to his wife, and the two shall become one flesh" (Mt 19:5-6). We are supposed to *leave* and *cleave* so that we can become *one*. We make our own new family. When speaking about "love as the principle and power of communion," Pope John Paul II told us in *Familiaris Consortio* that, "The first communion is the one which is established and which develops between husband and wife: by virtue of the covenant of married life, the man and woman 'are no longer two but one flesh' and they are called to grow continually in their communion through day-to-day fidelity to their marriage promise of total mutual self-giving" (*Familiaris Consortio*, 19).

Pope John Paul II's words remind us that husband and wife have made a *covenant* with one another, committing to fidelity each and every day, as well as a promise to give oneself totally to the spouse. Through our self-giving, our marriage blossoms and grows in holiness and maturity. It is through our daily activities and communion with each other that our commitment deepens, especially through the challenges that at times beset us.

The Catechism again reminds us, "Holy Scripture affirms that man and woman were created for one another: 'It is not good that the man should be alone.' The woman, 'flesh of his flesh,' i.e., his counterpart, his equal, his nearest in all things, is given to him by God as a 'helpmate'; she thus represents God from whom comes our help. 'Therefore a man leaves his father and his mother and cleaves to his wife, and they become one flesh.' The Lord himself shows that this signifies an unbreakable union of their two lives by recalling what the plan of the Creator has been 'in the beginning': 'So they are no longer two, but one flesh'" (CCC, 1605).

The sacrament of their marriage unites the couple in love, responsibility, sacrifice, and service to one another. Sometimes this union of hearts in all things may sound "easier said than done," if you know what I mean. However, a love that is authentic, devoted, strong, and sacrificial will see the couple through all of the bumps in the road that they will encounter throughout their lives. The couple's love will grow in strength to the extent that they will allow it to. Sacrifice and prayer are vital. Hopefully, the couple will have begun a prayer life together before they were married and will continue praying together morning and night to strengthen their marriage bond and draw them ever closer to God. If they aren't praying together on a regular basis they can't expect their marriage to blossom in the manner in which Our Lord would like. In the case of a prayerful wife and a not-so-prayerful husband, the wife can be an example, leading her husband closer to God. Her sacrifices and deep prayer will ultimately be what will bring him around. With a big grin on his face and a mischievous look in his eyes, my husband has told me on more than one occasion that God has put him in my life to make me a saint! I bet you know what he is implying!

Establishing habits of prayer will work wonders. Perhaps a wife will suggest that not only will they say their "Grace Before Meals" at the dinner table, but they will hold hands in bed after they've kissed one another "good night" and even pray an "Our Father" together as a couple – the start of evening prayer as *one*. Eventually, in time, a prayer habit is formed and other prayers and intentions are added

There may be times when reaching your hand over to join your husband's to pray may be more difficult than ever. You may have had a disagreement earlier in the day that has not yet been resolved. What better way than through prayer?

to their single "Our Father" prayed together in the evening. Remember that wise verse in Ephesians 4:26: "Don't let the sun go down on your anger"? There may be times when reaching your hand over to join your husband's to pray may be more difficult than ever. You may have had a disagreement earlier in the day that has not yet been resolved. What better way than through prayer?

A clever wife will also certainly find a way to be sure that she and her husband are united in prayer each morning, as well. Mornings can be very hectic, as every mother will attest, and morning prayers concurrently as a couple may sometimes be forgotten or delayed. My husband and I say our morning prayers together over the telephone. That works, too! He leaves very early in the morning for work, and I say my morning prayers alone, then again afterward at the breakfast table with the kids. My husband and I connect in prayer a little later on over the telephone. Couples can establish their own prayer lives with what works the best for them. Pope John Paul II has said that it doesn't matter how you pray, just be sure to pray! Prayer will keep a couple united in love.

A married Catholic couple is blessed with many graces through the sacrament of their marriage. The Catechism tells us, "From a valid marriage arises *a bond* between the spouses which, by its very nature is perpetual and exclusive; furthermore, in a Christian marriage the spouses are strengthened and, as it were, consecrated for the duties and the dignity of their state *by a special sacrament*" (CCC, 1638). A Catholic married couple can call upon the graces of their sacrament through their prayers together and can believe in their hearts that they will be strengthened by virtue of the fact that they have been united in a sacred bond when they crossed over the threshold into the sacrament of marriage. At times when an outside situation challenges us, I will remind my husband before we pray, "Our prayers are powerful – we can call upon the graces from the sacrament of our marriage," and we are given the opportunity to pray together with extra hope and strength to tackle the problem. We have to trust and believe it!

"'By reason of their state in life and of their order, [Christian spouses] have their own special gifts in the People of God.' This grace proper to the sacrament of matrimony is intended to perfect the couple's love and to strengthen their indissoluble unity. By this grace they 'help one another to attain holiness in their married life and in the welcoming and educating their children'" (CCC, 1641; *Lumen Gentium*).

Isn't it wonderful to know that our holy Mother Church assures us of the graces that we will receive and also reminds us that in receiving these graces when we ask for them in prayer, we will be strengthened in our unity and be enabled to help our spouse to attain holiness? I just love God's plan! In living out our state of life faithfully, we are given graces to become holy!

In *Gaudium et Spes* (The Church in the Modern World), we learn, "Just as of old God encountered his people with a covenant of love and fidelity, so our Savior, the spouse of the Church, now encounters Christian spouses through the sacrament of matrimony." The Catechism tells us, "Christ dwells with them, gives them the strength to take up their crosses and so follow him, to rise again after they have fallen, to forgive one another, to bear one another's burdens, to 'be subject to one another out of reverence for Christ,' and to love one another with supernatural, tender, and fruitful love. In the joys of their love and family life he gives them here on earth a foretaste of the wedding feast of the Lamb" (CCC,1642; Eph 5:21; cf. Gal 6:2).

We are truly blessed! Christ himself gives us strength for the journey – strength to overcome *anything* in our marriages! We need only ask him for it and devote ourselves to him and our spouse. In this way, we will have a stronger eagerness to pick up our crosses and bear with the annoyances and tribulations we face on a day-to-day basis. We will know in the depths of our hearts that what we do to one another, we do to Christ, as Blessed Teresa of Calcutta so poignantly and continually professed, and which we have learned from the Gospel of Matthew (25: 31- 46) and know is critical to our Christian marriage.

1. *What do you think are some of the attributes that a Christian married couple emanates?*

_____

_____

_____

_____

_____

_____

_____

2. *Where can a Christian married couple find the strength to withstand the wear and tear from everyday life in this world?*

_____

_____

_____

_____

_____

_____

_____

_____

3. How are the husband and wife united in love? What can help them to strengthen their bond of love? List at least three things that will help:

_____

_____

_____

_____

_____

_____

_____

4. What are some ways in which a wife can be instrumental in including prayer in her and her husband's daily lives?

_____

_____

_____

_____

_____

_____

_____

_____

PART TWO 🔥 DIFFERENCES AND COMPLIMENTARITY

"Love for his wife as mother of his children and love for the

children themselves are for the man the natural

way of understanding and fulfilling his own fatherhood."

– Familiaris Consortio, 25

Let's get into some of the nitty-gritty everyday issues regarding men and women. When you look in the mirror, do you see your husband? Of course not, unless he's standing there with you. We are not clones of our husbands, nor should we want to be. We certainly do not want them to be clones of us! Please allow me to also clarify something else: Men are not from Mars and women are not from Venus. However, we do know that men and women are similar in some respects – and very different in others.

It's a no-brainer to recognize that there are major physical differences between men and women. However, it is so interesting to note that scientists have discovered that there are also differences in the anatomy of men's and women's brains and in how their brains work. I find it very interesting that men and women use different parts of their brains to accomplish the same task. Men's brains are larger, but women's brains have more gray matter and have more intricate communications between brain cells, especially in the frontal cortex which is the area involved in judgment and decision making. Women's brains may work more efficiently with a higher rate of blood flow. No, I'm not sneakily trying to imply that women are more intelligent! I am pointing out some basic and interesting differences in how men and women may view situations and how they may be wired to respond to stimuli around them.

Testing has revealed that women are more verbal and communicate more effectively, while men are better at tasks such as negotiating through a three-dimensional space or rotating an object in their minds mentally through three dimensions. Women have the ability to multitask or concentrate on a number of things at once, while men prefer to, and are more able to, concentrate on one task at a time or focus on a single goal. But multitasking is not necessarily always the most efficient or safest way to operate, for instance, in the case of talking on a cell phone while driving a vehicle, when a matter of seconds can mean life or death.

An interesting discovery on a primitive sort of level is that a man's brain at rest is most ready to achieve instant activity or to physically respond to stimulus. A woman's basal resting state is more attuned to differences in expression and communication. This may relate to the fact that a man is stronger physically, is a protector, ready to respond to physical threat in the night to protect his family. On the other hand, a woman is more attune with her children's needs in the night because she is a nurturer.

Let's look at a few points of interest on this topic of differences and similarities. Husband and wife hopefully are in the same boat when it comes to wanting what is best for their family. When speaking of emotionally stable individuals, we know that both men and women are capable of caring and loving and also of receiving love and care in return. Oftentimes though, their love will be shown in different and various ways. A father may want to toss his small child up playfully and catch him or her safely in his arms, spinning his child around gently, while oodles of giggles are exuberantly expressed from his little tot. Mother, on the other hand, may prefer to cuddle and rock her child while singing him a nursery rhyme or reading her a story as she nestles her soft face against her mother's chest. Both forms of affection are indeed loving and come from the heart. No form is better than the other; both are important to a growing child.

I'm not intending to stereotype at all, but a husband is usually a bit more "rough and tumble" and interested in guy kind of stuff like hanging out in the garage or shed, while the mother is more of a nurturer and may express her love in a "softer" manner for the most part. She is interested in "feathering her nest" and watching over her household. This is not to say that the roles cannot be reversed at times, but, generally speaking, I think you will agree that men and women operate differently. Sometimes you may even wonder if you have another kid in the house – but in a grown man's body! I'm sure that there are times when you ask your husband to calm down and not get too rough with the kids or get them all "wound up" before bedtime! It's the protective mother in you being sure that everyone is safe and comfortable.

Loving and Communicating

Can husband and wife clash in their parenting and "spousing" styles? You bet they can! I'm sure you are well aware. When do the differences between man and woman pose a threat or cause some discomfort or conflict? Perhaps it is when there is a lack of communication in some areas of their relationship. Other times, maybe when there may be misunderstandings. Men and women think differently. We women may think that men only see black and white while women can see black, white, and gray.

Men want to fix things immediately. Women may want to discuss the situation in more depth and come up with a plan to fix the problem. That's not to say that a woman can't be quick in her decisions or swift in solving a problem. A man, however, may feel impatient and want to cut to the chase when a woman is expressing herself, and the woman may feel that she is not being listened to – at all! All kinds of misunderstandings can develop. Neither person is wrong in his or her thinking, yet at times frustration rears its head because we are not sure how to respond or confused about how we feel. However, patience is vital and will help the couple to pause and listen to each other before jumping to conclusions. Because we are human beings and we can get tired and cranky, this is one reason to possibly postpone an important discussion and schedule it for a more appropriate time – when the two of you are calmer and more rested, and better able to practice the heroic virtues that will keep peace in your marriage.

Recognizing that a man's self-worth is central to how he feels and how he responds to various situations is very important for a woman because it will help her to understand her man. Similarly, acknowledging that a woman wants to feel protected, secure, and appreciated is helpful for a man, as well. Earlier, I mentioned a mirror. What do you think your husband sees in your face during your discussions with him? What are you mirroring back to him? Is it acceptance of his role in your family unit and of his input in family decisions? Does he see worry, concern, or rejection in your face or hear it in your voice? If so, hopefully he will want to talk with you about it when he senses that something may be wrong. If he doesn't initiate the conversation, you of course may bring it up.

You may also want to consider what your unspoken words are conveying. Maybe you are having a hard time some days expressing that you truly appreciate the hard work that your husband does to provide for his family. Or you may not realize how important it is for your husband to know that you are appreciative. However, he may need to actually hear you tell him at times, to give his confidence a boost. Perhaps you are upset about something, and you're not sure how to express it. Banging around pots and pans may draw attention to yourself, but it will not solve the problem! Another sort of communication, the "silent treatment," or trying to make your husband suffer

Does he see worry, concern, or rejection in your face or hear it in your voice? If so, hopefully he will want to talk with you about it when he senses that something may be wrong. If he doesn't initiate the conversation, you of course may bring it up.

while you sulk because you feel hurt, should be avoided and is not a recommended practice for a happy marriage. If there is a temptation to resort to sulking, pray instead and ask Our Lord for grace and strength to approach your husband in open communication about what is bothering you. Many wives find that most of the time their husbands are unaware that they have caused hurt feelings. Your husband will want to know so that it can be cleared up and you can move on. St. Francis de Sales once said, "When you encounter difficulties and contradictions, don't try to break them, but bend them with gentleness and time." Prayer, gentleness, and time work wonders.

"Love Is Patient"

Read the very beautiful passage in 1 Corinthians 13: 1-13. We've read it more times than we can count. We've heard it read at so many wedding ceremonies, yet it remains poignant and profound and tugs at our heart each time we hear it. We can strive to live by this passage. I have it framed on my bedroom wall.

A good habit for a husband and wife is to set aside a convenient regular time to discuss what they have on their minds, thus keeping the doors of communication open wide. You may want to have a regular weekly meeting of the minds. You can keep things light.

Discuss household topics and issues that have come up throughout the week with the children. You can talk about projects that you want to accomplish around the house, the schedule, the budget – basically bringing each other up to date with all kinds of stuff that affects your lives. During this little meeting, you may also bring up a misunderstanding or perhaps a hurt feeling. Ask your husband to please listen to what you have to say before he gives you his input. Afterwards, you listen quietly to what he has to say and see what you can work out together – give-and-take. We have to learn to become very good listeners and avoid the temptation to jump in to defend our point of view while our spouse is expressing his, and we ask that he does the same for us. I think that if we regard our marriage as a 150-150 partnership, rather than a "fifty-fifty" one, then we are on the right track. If we are willing to give more than "our share," then we are really giving. We must keep in mind that throughout our marriage there will be times when one spouse gives more of themselves than the other for a variety of reasons, whether it is due to one spouse's deficiency in physical, emotional, or psychological areas, either temporary or permanently.

Oftentimes, I know exactly what my husband is going to say before he opens his mouth. This happens so often that my husband says it's scary! Is it because he is so predictable, or because we are united with each other? I like to think it is because we are united in love and understand each other. Other times, his way of thinking or reacting to a situation may puzzle me, because I would not have expected it. That's typically when it is yet again clear to me that men are not women – that we are not identical and that we will have our own opinions and perspectives. I can't expect him to think like a woman. If I want a woman's point of view, I can call my sisters, a friend, or in years past, my mother. However, it would not be to talk about my husband, because that would not be fair or proper.

When we are not seeing "eye-to-eye," it's a great time to pause and really try to listen to my spouse's point of view, a great opportunity for learning something new about my husband and about myself, a time for selfless love and a greater openness. It is a chance to trust and surrender to my "other half." We can find a healthy balance in our relationships; we can indeed take heart that "there is no fear in love, but perfect love casts out all fear" (1 Jn 4:18).

As partners to our husbands, we should pray to discern his feelings about his sense of worth and do all we can to be sure that he feels accepted and respected in our relationship. If we are feeling unappreciated or misunderstood, it's time to talk about it with our husband. When there is a need to talk things out, no time is better than the present so that things won't "stew" or "fester" and become worse or seemingly insurmountable. Naturally, there may be times when we decide to hold off on a discussion so that we can have the privacy to talk and express our feelings to one another, perhaps when the children are in bed, and also maybe to cool down, ponder, and pray first.

United for the Children's Sake

Regarding the children, very important is the need for husband and wife to form a united front and be committed to it in dealings with the children, so the children will feel secure and also know that their parents mean what they say. If the mother is saying one thing and the father another, the children will be confused. Family rules and parameters keep children safe and help them to feel loved. Husbands and wives must work at achieving a union of minds even through their differences of opinion in presenting what is best for their children. This may not always be an easy task in every household. However, every attempt to present a sincere, united front with the children is a step in the right direction together as a family.

We must resist the temptation to make rash decisions or disciplines regarding the children. If we blurt out something to the children when we may be frustrated, it won't be easy to take it back when we realize that we weren't being fair. Of course a parent can apologize to his or her child, but hurtful words can really sting and are not easily forgotten. Children will not be able to learn stability and responsibility very well with "wishy-washy" rules either – when something is said and then not followed through. The only thing they will learn in that case is that mommy doesn't say what she means or mean what she says. Let's be sure to confer with our husbands about major decisions. We also need to make time to establish ground rules beforehand, so we will be ready to handle the situation.

Learning to communicate lovingly and acknowledging our differences and the fact that man and woman have their own specific gifts to bring to their marriage and family will help to alleviate some anxiety and confusion. It will also help us to be more accepting of one another. Prayer, as often as is possible, will cement our relationships. Let's try to keep a sense of humor, which can go a long way and act as a healing balm. Let us also recall that our marriage is a work in progress. We are not saints yet! I love what St. Francis de Sales said: "Be patient with everyone, but above all with yourself. Do not lose courage in considering your own imperfections but instantly set about remedying them – every day begin the task anew."

1. List some attributes of women:

_____

_____

_____

_____

_____

_____

2. List some attributes or qualities of men:

_____

_____

_____

_____

_____

_____

3. What are some areas where husband and wife may not agree?

_____

_____

_____

_____

_____

_____

4. *What are some strategies for good communication between spouses?*

_____

_____

_____

_____

_____

5. *List at least three reasons why husband and wife should present a united front in raising the children:*

_____

_____

_____

_____

_____

6. *What are the keys for loving service to one's spouse and for marital happiness?*

_____

_____

_____

_____

_____

Summing Up

You and your husband have entered a covenant of love, a partnership filled with joys and challenges. Holy Mother Church tells us that we are free and able to call upon the graces of the sacrament of our marriage to receive strength and help us to live out our marital vows. Prayer is our saving grace. We should be sure to plan times for prayer with our spouses so that we can remain united in love and strength.

God has called each family to holiness. Our responses to one another in our families will be a means to our sanctification. Pope John Paul II reminded us in *Familiaris Consortio* that "Each family finds within itself a summons that cannot be ignored, and that specifies both its dignity and its responsibility: Family, *become* what you *are*." We have a very high calling and we must acknowledge it and move forward, one foot in front of the other each day, serving one another in our families and also setting an example for the world.

Thoughts to Ponder

While we may be madly in love with our husbands, they may be driving us mad at the same time! I am teasingly pointing out that husbands and wives are very different, physically and emotionally, but they complement one another and actually need one another to be complete.

Husbands and wives need to practice the heroic virtues for peace and harmony within their home. They must bear with one another patiently and strive to be understanding of their differences. They should learn to communicate lovingly and realize that their commitment to each other means sacrificial and extreme love. Marriage means a full surrender to one's spouse.

We will be in a very good place in our marriage if we can focus on the fact that "love is patient; love is kind; love is not envious or boastful or arrogant or rude. It does not insist on its own way; it is not irritable or resentful; it does not rejoice in wrongdoing, but rejoices in the truth. It bears all things, believes all things, hopes all things, endures all things. Love never ends" (I Cor 13).

Dear Lord,

Thank you for the gift of my marriage. Please help me to be ever mindful of my husband's and my responsibility before you. Help us to be strong in our battle against the evil in the culture that surrounds us and touches us in one way or another each day. Please grant us the graces that we need most. Help me to be a better wife so that my husband and I may come ever closer to you and our family may truly glorify your name! Please remind me with every beat of my heart that "love never ends."

Amen.

Prayer

3. The Nursery:
The Blessings of Little Souls

"...But Jesus said,

'Let the children come

to me, and do not

prevent them;

for the kingdom of

heaven belongs

to such as these.'"

~ Mt 19:14

Part One ❧ Open to the Gift of Life: Our "Human and Christian Responsibility"

*"God blessed them, and God said to them,
'Be fruitful and multiply, and fill the earth and subdue it.'"*
– Gen 1:28

Nothing can compare to the overwhelming and phenomenal feeling of a mother who has been handed her newborn babe immediately after giving birth, as he or she lies against her heart, to caress and hold for the very first time. Similarly, the adoptive mother, who after much waiting at last holds her new baby or child in her arms, is overcome with deep joy. A child is a precious gift and blessing: There is absolutely no doubt about that!

We learn from *Familiaris Consortio*, "With the creation of man and woman in his own image and likeness, God crowns and brings to perfection the work of his hands: He calls them to a special sharing in his love and in his power as Creator and Father, through their free and responsible cooperation in transmitting the gift of human life.... Thus the fundamental task of the family is to serve life, to actualize in history the original blessing of the Creator – that of transmitting by procreation the divine image from person to person." Imagine that! God cooperates with husband and wife to create human life! It is "the work of his hands" through us! So, in reality, there are three working together to create human life: the mother, the father, and God! When Christian parents cooperate with the divine, Our Lord is pleased.

We read in Genesis 5:1-3, "When God created humankind; he made them in the likeness of God. Male and female he created them, and he blessed them and named them 'humankind' when they were created."

Sadly, we live in a world where life is not necessarily valued everywhere as precious and unrepeatable. Our society is sadly a throwaway society – if it's broken, we throw it out. We know that in the case of human life, tragically it is also often regarded in the same way. Doctors who are supposed to preserve lives often advise parents to abort a baby when they feel the baby may be defective in some way. Human embryos are harvested for science and to produce babies, and many of them are destroyed in the process – just thrown away as waste! The elderly and terminally ill are viewed as worthless by some when they cease to be "productive." Large Christian families today are often looked down upon, and the parents are even accused of overpopulating the earth by a society that promotes the convenient and standardized one- or two-child family unit.

We read in the Catechism, "So the Church, which 'is on the side of life,' teaches that 'each and every marriage act must remain open to the transmission of life.' This particular doctrine, expounded upon on numerous occasions by the magisterium, is based on the inseparable connection, established by God, which man on his own initiative may not break, between the unitive significance and the procreative significance which are both inherent to the marriage act" (*Humanae Vitae*, 12; cf. Pius XI, *Casti connubii*).

Yet again, Mother Church upholds the dignity of every person when she says, "But the Church firmly believes that human life, even if weak and suffering is always a splendid gift of God's goodness. Against the pessimism and selfishness which cast a shadow over the world, the Church stands for life: in each human life she sees the splendor of that 'Yes,' that 'Amen,' who is Christ himself. To the 'No' which assails and afflicts the world, she replies with the living, 'Yes,' thus defending the human person and the world from all who plot against it and harm life.

"The Church is called upon to manifest anew to everyone, with clear and stronger conviction, her will to promote human life by every means and to defend it against all attacks, in whatever condition or state of development it is found" (*Familiaris Consortio*). These are powerful and beautiful words. The Church stands for life – always!

Therefore, even though a mother's role may not always be viewed as valuable by our society, Catholic mothers can feel encouraged, knowing that our Church supports them in their high vocation of motherhood. Moreover, Our Lord himself calls them to a "special sharing in his love and in his power as Creator and Father!" (*Familiaris Consortio*).

Unfortunately, not every mother is aware of her God-given dignity and gifts or the support from her Church and may even feel confused because of what she hears from the culture.

Mothers are encouraged to be open to their responsibility to new life in yet another Church document, *Gaudium et Spes*, which tells us, "Called to give life, spouses share in the creative power and fatherhood of God (cf. Eph 3:14; Mt 23:9). 'Married couples should regard it as their proper mission to transmit human life and to educate their children; they should realize that they are thereby *cooperating with* the love of *God the Creator* and are, in a certain sense, its interpreters. They will fulfill this duty with a sense of human and Christian responsibility.'"

Let's be sure that we mothers realize that we have been given the gift and the privilege of partnership with God to create human life! Through the love of the husband and wife, Our Lord comes into the marital embrace and brings forth life. This is a concept almost too magnificent to ponder! But we must cooperate with life and the love of God and not deter life in any way. Blessed Teresa of Calcutta refers to life as the most beautiful gift of God. She has told us, "Let us bring peace into the world, by love and compassion, by respecting life, the most beautiful gift of God. Let us love each person – the unborn, the young, the old, the sick and the poor – with the same love with which God loves each one of us, a tender and personal love."

The Bedroom: "Cooperators in the Love of God the Creator"

Some essential teachings of our Church regarding a husband and wife's cooperation with God to transmit human life can be found in *Familiaris Consortio*. I encourage couples to read this letter in its entirety and refer to it often, for it holds much wisdom, insight, and guidance for the Christian couple. It can be found at Catholic bookstores and on the Vatican Web site: http://www.vatican.va.

"Fecundity is the fruit and the signs of conjugal love, the living testimony of the full reciprocal self-giving of the spouses: 'While not making the other purposes of matrimony of less account, the true practice of the conjugal love, and the whole meaning of the family life which results from it, have this aim: that the couple be ready with stout hearts to cooperate with the love of the Creator and the Savior, who through them will enlarge and enrich his own family day by day'" (FC, 28).

Conception and Contraception

A big temptation in our day is to use contraceptives, or artificial means, to prevent pregnancies. Newly married couples may feel that it is perfectly acceptable to decide to put off having children until they are more established financially, and they may even fear bringing children into a corrupted or dismal world. Some couples are under the impression that the birth control pill prevents pregnancies, when it in fact can serve as a potential abortifacient. This means that the pill can actually kill the conceived child (the fertilized egg) by making the womb uninhabitable for the newly conceived life.

We live in an era when there are so many artificial means available to prevent pregnancies and are sadly even prescribed by Catholic doctors. If I had listened to the advice of my doctor, my daughter Mary-Catherine would not have been born! He advised me to have my tubes tied after my fourth Cesarean section, telling me that there was a chance that my uterus would rupture if I were to become pregnant again. Beware of doctors who tell you these kinds of things when you are in a vulnerable position, such as on a medical table with your feet up in the stirrups, or as you are being wheeled into surgery when you may be drugged and also don't have time to think. I adamantly refused my doctor's recommendation to tie my tubes. I was completely healthy and in no danger. My doctor was covering himself legally, I feel. I am not suggesting that you should endanger your life. However, I am saying that we must be prudent, prayerful, and follow our Church's teachings – always.

If I had listened to the advice of my doctor, my daughter Mary-Catherine would not have been born.... Beware of doctors who tell you these kinds of things when you are in a vulnerable position....

An Antifamily Mentality

Our culture suggests that we should hold off bringing children into the marriage for many reasons and also encourages couples to limit the size of their families. I love what Blessed Teresa has said about children. She said, "How can there be too many children? That's like saying there are too many flowers."

Pope John Paul II discussed some of the pertinent issues that Christian married couples face regarding family planning in *Familiaris Consortio* when he said, "Scientific and technical progress, which contemporary man is continually expanding in his dominion over nature, not only offers the hope of creating a new and better humanity, but also causes even greater anxiety regarding the future. Some ask themselves if it is a good thing to be alive or if it would be better never to have been born; they doubt therefore if it is right to bring others into life when perhaps they will curse their existence in a cruel world with unforeseeable terrors. Others consider themselves to be the only ones for whom the advantages of technology are intended and they exclude others by imposing on them contraceptives or even worse means. Still others, imprisoned in a consumer mentality and whose sole concern is to bring about a continual growth of material goods, finish by ceasing to understand, and thus by refusing, the spiritual riches of a new human life. The ultimate reason for these mentalities is the absence of people's hearts of God, whose love alone is stronger than all the world's fears and can conquer them.

"Thus the antilife mentality is born, as can be seen in many current issues: one thinks, for example, of a certain panic deriving from the studies of ecologists and futurologists on population growth, which sometimes exaggerate the danger of demographic increase to the quality of life.

"But the Church firmly believes that all human life, even if weak and suffering, is always a splendid gift of God's goodness. Against pessimism and selfishness which cast a shadow over the world, the Church stands for life: in each human life she sees the splendor of that "Yes," that "Amen," who is Christ himself. To the "no" which assails and afflicts the world, she replies with this living "Yes," thus defending the human person and the world from all who plot against and harm life.

"The Church is called upon to manifest anew to everyone, with clear and stronger conviction, her will to promote human life by every means and to defend it against all attacks, in whatever condition or state of development it is found.

"Thus the Church condemns as a grave offense against human dignity and justice all those activities of governments or other public authorities which attempt to limit in any way the freedom of couples in deciding about children. Consequently any violence *applied* by such authorities in favor of contraception or, still worse, of sterilization and procured abortion, must be altogether condemned and forcefully rejected. Likewise to be denounced as gravely unjust are cases where, in international relations, economic help is given for the advancement of peoples is made conditional on programs of contraception, sterilization, and procured abortion" (*Familiaris Consortio*, 30).

To further understand the Church's teaching about her view on contraceptives, we need only read what Pope John Paul II teaches us in *Evangelium Vitae* (The Gospel of Life), "It is frequently asserted that *contraception*, if made safe and available to all, is the most effective remedy against abortion. The Catholic Church is then accused of actually promoting abortion, because she obstinately continues to teach the moral unlawfulness of contraception. When looked at carefully, this objection is clearly unfounded. It may be that many people use contraception with a view to excluding the subsequent temptation of abortion. But the negative values inherent in the 'contraceptive mentality' – which is very different from responsible parenthood, lived in respect for the full truth of the conjugal act – are such that they in fact strengthen this temptation when an unwanted life is conceived. Indeed, the proabortion culture is especially strong precisely where the Church's teaching on contraception is rejected. Certainly, from the moral point of view contraception and abortion are *specifically different* evils: the former contradicts the full truth of the sexual act as the proper expression of conjugal love, while the latter destroys the life of a human being; the former is opposed to the virtue of chastity in marriage, the latter is opposed to the virtue of justice and directly violates the divine commandment 'You shall not kill'" *(Evangelium Vitae,* 13).

The Bible speaks of contraception. We can read in Galatians 5:19-21, "Now the works of the flesh are obvious: fornication, impurity, licentiousness, idolatry, sorcery, enmities, strife, jealousy, anger, quarrels, dissensions, factions, envy, drunkenness, carousing, and things like these. I am warning you as I warned you before: those who do such things will not inherit the kingdom of God." (The word "sorcery" is translated as *pharmakedia,* which means taking herbs to prevent pregnancy. Today that means the use of medications and other means to prevent pregnancy.) This reading clearly warns us of the outcome for people participating in these acts.

What Is Permissible for Family Planning?

The Catechism tells us, "Periodic continence, that is, the methods of birth regulation based on self-observation and the use of infertile periods, is in conformity with the objective criteria of morality. These methods respect the bodies of the spouses, encourage tenderness between them, and favor the education of an authentic freedom. In contrast, 'every action which, whether in anticipation of the conjugal act, or in its accomplishment, or in the development of its natural consequences, proposes, whether as an end or as a means, render procreation impossible' is intrinsically evil:

> *Thus the innate language that expresses the total reciprocal self-giving of husband and wife is overlaid, through contraception, by an objectively contradictory language, namely, that of not giving oneself totally to the other. This leads not only to a positive refusal to be open to life but also a falsification of the inner truth of conjugal love, which is called upon to give itself in personal totality.... The difference, both anthropological and moral, between contraception and recourse to the rhythm of the cycle...involves in the final analysis two irreconcilable concepts of the human person and of human sexuality"* (Familiaris Consortio).

I recommend that both married couples and engaged couples read the Catechism together, particularly No. 2360, "The Love of Husband and Wife," to further understand the Church's teachings regarding Christian families. Other relevant Church documents to read and study are: *Casti Connubii* (Christian Marriage) by Pope Pius XI, *Humanae Vitae* by Pope Paul VI, and *Familiaris Consortio* and *Mulieris Dignitatem* by Pope John Paul II.

It would be wonderful to keep a copy of the Catechism nearby in the kitchen, dining room, or bedroom for those impromptu or planned discussions with your husband. In the case of a newly married couple, discussions about intimacy in their marriage and their responsibility to be cooperative with God's plan regarding their future children can come up at the dinner table, traveling together, or anywhere. The wife may initially bring up the subject by reading from the Catechism as a conversation starter. Or the couple may plan to sit down together at a particular time to educate themselves further in Church teaching. A prayer said together, followed by reading from one of the above documents would be a very fine initiative. Please also find a spiritual advisor who is directly in line with the magisterium of our Church.

Natural Family Planning

Natural family planning (NFP) is the approved method of the Catholic Church for spacing children. The *Modern Catholic Dictionary* by Father John Hardon, SJ, the late renowned author and theologian, defines natural family planning as "the controlling of human conception by restricting the marital act to the infertile periods of the wife. This practice is based on the theory that the period of a woman's ovulation can be determined with considerable accuracy. A variety of methods, or their combination, is used to determine the period of ovulation. From the moral standpoint, natural family planning is permissible. As stated by Pope Paul VI: 'If there are serious motives to space out births, which derive from physical or psychological conditions of husband or wife, or from external conditions, it is licit to take account of the natural rhythms inherent in the generative functions'" *(Humanae Vitae* II, 16).

There are a variety of methods of natural family planning, and married and engaged couples should seek qualified instructors through the Church to learn the methods. It's a good idea for an engaged couple to study and learn the method of reading a woman's fertility signs prior to their marriage. This is also a time when the soon-to-be wife and husband can discuss the care of their babies.

I sincerely hope that engaged and married Catholic women will consider breast-feeding their babies so as to gain many benefits from the colostrum, which is the first milk from the mother's breast after a baby is born, providing the antibodies, nourishment, and a loving bond between mother and baby, as well as an amazing and very natural way to space out the children.

According to author Sheila Kippley, a well-known expert on natural family planning, "NFP is a way of following God's plan for achieving and/or avoiding pregnancy. It consists of ways to achieve or to avoid pregnancy using the physical means that God has built into human nature." She states, "NFP consists of two distinct forms:

1. **Ecological breast-feeding:** This is a form of child care that normally spaces babies about two years apart on the average.

2. **Systematic NFP:** This is a system that uses a woman's signs of fertility to determine the fertile and infertile times of her cycle."

Couples seeking to avoid pregnancy practice "chaste abstinence during the fertile time of her cycle" (taken from http://www. nfpandmore.org, which is a great resource for Catholic couples).

The Many Benefits of Breast-feeding

"Yet it was you who took me from the womb;

you kept me safe on my mother's breast." – Ps 22:9

I breast-fed all of my babies until they were toddlers. Breast-feeding is a very beautiful plan from God to nourish our children, bond with them, and space out our pregnancies. I am often asked how I was able to space my children in the way that I did. Breast-feeding worked as a natural child spacer for me. Of course, there are many wonderful benefits to breast-feeding other than natural child spacing. I have always recommended this form of infant feeding when possible. Adoptive mothers do not have much choice in this regard.

Some of the other benefits of breast-feeding are the physical ones. Babies who are breast-fed are found to be more intelligent, healthier, with less chance of developing common illnesses because of the antibodies that are given through the breast milk and the sucking that is required on the babies' part to nurse. This sucking helps to prevent ear infections, develops the baby's dental arch, and even its facial features. In addition, breast-fed children are proven to be happy and stable even later in life. I recommend Sheila Kippley's book, *Breastfeeding and Catholic Motherhood,* for a more in-depth look at the spiritual and physical benefits of breast-feeding your babies.

I also highly recommend the La Leche League International for assistance and support with breast-feeding. Their helpline phone number is (877) 452-5324, and their Web site is: www.llli.org.

I find it wonderful that our Church has upheld and supported Catholic motherhood. Many may not be aware of some of our popes' words of encouragement in this regard. Popes Gregory the Great, Benedict XIV, Pius XII, and John Paul II have all supported breast-feeding. Additionally, The Pontifical Academy of Sciences held a conference in 1995 entitled "Breast-feeding: Science and Society" in which Pope John Paul II addressed the study session. He said, "[The known benefit of breast-feeding] is obviously a matter of concern to countless women and children, and something that clearly has general importance for every society, rich or poor. One hopes that your studies will serve to heighten public awareness of how much this natural activity benefits the child and helps to create the closeness and maternal bonding so necessary for healthy child development. So human and natural is this bond that the Psalms use the image of the infant at its mother's breast as a picture of God's care for man (cf. Ps. 22:9). So vital is this interaction between mother and child that my predecessor, Pope Pius XII, urged all Catholic mothers, if at all possible, to nourish their children themselves."

Pope John Paul II has also said, "In normal circumstances [the advantages of breast-feeding] include two major benefits to the child: protection against disease and proper nourishment. Moreover, in addition to these [benefits], this natural way of feeding can create a bond of love and security between mother and child, and enable the child to assert its presence as a person through interaction with the mother.

All of this is a matter of immediate concern…. From various perspectives, therefore, this is of interest to the Church, called as she is to concern herself with the sanctity of life and the family…. In practical terms what we are saying is that mothers need time, information, and support…. So much is expected of women in many societies that time to devote to breast-feeding and early care is not always available …[yet] no one can substitute for the mother in this natural activity…" (pp.35, 36, from an address to the Pontificiae Academiae Scientarium and the Royal Society, 1995).

God alone knows the future. Accepting the new gift of life in marriage should never be delayed without sufficiently serious reasons. You may refer to *Humanae Vitae* (10, 16) for more information about Church teaching in this regard. Delaying conception for frivolous reasons means standing in the way of God's plan for the particular human being that he wants to bring into the world. Couples are encouraged to seek out a holy priest or religious whom they can feel comfortable with to talk about their concerns in this regard.

Let us reflect on these words about welcoming life in our domestic churches from Pope John Paul II: "As the domestic church, the family is summoned to proclaim, celebrate, and serve the Gospel of life. This is a responsibility which first concerns married couples, called to be givers of life, on the basis of an ever greater awareness of the meaning of procreation as a unique event which clearly reveals that human life is a gift received in order then to be given as a gift. In giving origin to a new life, parents recognize that the child 'as the fruit of their mutual gift of love, is, in turn, a gift for both of them, a gift which flows from them'" (*Evangelium Vitae*).

1. Why does being a faithful Catholic usually mean living in contradiction to our society with regards to accepting the gift of life?

_____

_____

_____

_____

_____

_____

2. What does humankind consist of? (Gn 5:1-3)

_____

_____

_____

_____

_____

_____

3. What are the two significances that were mentioned that are
inherent to the marriage act?

_____

_____

_____

_____

_____

4. Why must a married couple utilize the natural rhythm of the
human body to plan their family rather than by artificial means?

_____

_____

_____

_____

Part Two ✒ A Special Communion with the
Mystery of Life

"Motherhood involves a special communion with the mystery of life, as it develops in the woman's womb. The mother is filled with wonder at this mystery of life, and 'understands' with unique intuition what is happening inside her. In the light of the 'beginning,' the mother accepts and loves as a person the child she is carrying in her womb. This unique contact with the new human being developing within her gives rise to an attitude towards human beings – not only towards her own child, but every human being – which profoundly marks the woman's personality. It is commonly thought that *women are more capable than men of paying attention to another person*, and that motherhood develops this predisposition even more. The man – even with all his sharing in parenthood – always remains 'outside' the process of pregnancy and the baby's birth; in many ways he has to *learn* his own '*fatherhood' from the mother*. One can say that this is part of the normal human dimension of parenthood, including the stages that follow the birth of the baby, especially the initial period. The child's upbringing, taken as a whole, should include the contribution of both parents: the maternal and paternal contribution. In any event, the mother's contribution is decisive in laying the foundation for a new human personality" (*Mulieris Dignitatem*).

It's amazing when we consider the extraordinary role that mothers have been given in their vocation of bringing children into the world and to their families. Whether it occurs biologically or through adoption, a mother's contribution in the early stages of her child's life is "decisive in laying the foundation for a new human personality," as Pope John Paul II told us in *Mulieris Dignitatem*. Amazing! Yet, as a mother trudges through her days in the care of the home and family, she may not be exactly *feel* extraordinary, or that she is profoundly contributing to the early life of her offspring, or "decisive in laying the foundation for a new personality." That's because a mother's work can feel so ordinary and un-amazing a lot of the time. We mothers do what we do because we love. It's so nice to feel affirmed by Pope John Paul II's words regarding our role as mothers, which helps us to realize the great significance of our purpose.

In the case of the biological mother, she is truly "filled with wonder" and she joyfully experiences the blessing of her unborn baby as she intuitively understands this holy mystery that is happening to her, according to Pope John Paul II. A mother's love increases as her child grows within her and as God gifts her with motherly graces, causing her heart to expand to love other human beings in a deeper way as well. Therefore, we begin to see motherhood on a level that is intrinsically and spiritually so much more than changing diapers, late night feedings, and teenaged angst. Mothers have within their power the ability, by God's grace, to mold a human person's conscience and personality!

A Joyful Song

Faithful mothers make a joyful song to the Lord by virtue of rooting their vocation in love. Children bring deep joy to a mother's heart and soul, and she in turn offers back her work in the care of the family joyfully as a gift to the Lord. Blessed Teresa of Calcutta has said, "Joy is a net of love by which you can catch souls." It reminds me a little bit of the saying "You can catch more flies with honey than vinegar." A mother's joyful demeanor will be contagious and help to bring happiness to the family.

The exciting news that a gift of new life has been conceived within the mother's body is blessed and joyous music for the soul indeed! This one new unique and unrepeatable life actually changes the world forever.

Pope John Paul II has told us, "Acceptance, love, esteem, many-sided and united material, emotional, educational and spiritual concern for every child that comes into this world should always constitute a distinctive, essential characteristic of all Christians, in particular of the Christian family: thus children, while they are able to grow 'in wisdom and in stature, and in favor with God and man,' offer their own precious contribution to building to the family community and even to the sanctification of their parents" (*Familiaris Consortio*). Let us mothers remember Pope John Paul II's words about our own sanctification being offered through our children when we are dealing with some of the trials and tribulations in the household – cranky toddlers and teenaged angst, for instance! Our sanctification is woven in with our responses to our family.

Again we are reminded of spiritual help from our children in the Catechism: "Children in turn contribute to the *growth in* holiness of the parents" (CCC, 2227). I find it so beautiful and amazing to know that children actually help their parents in their sanctification process! Without our dear children, where would we be? What choices would we have made in life? Our children help us to stay on the

Our sanctification is woven in with our responses to our family. Again we are reminded of spiritual help from our children in the Catechism: "Children in turn contribute to the growth in holiness of the parents."

straight and narrow. I often think about how my children have helped to guide me in my vocation of motherhood. This may seem paradoxical, but it is so very true. Mothers are given the task and responsibility of raising their little souls to heaven and while doing so, the children will, by God's grace, also be helping to sanctify their parents' lives. A pretty nice arrangement from Our Lord, I would say!

I would like to end our reflection on the blessing of little souls with some poignant words from Pope John Paul II, who truly had a deep and brilliant understanding of the human heart. He said, "The eternal mystery of generation, which is in God himself, the one and Triune God (cf. Eph 3:14-15), is reflected in the woman's motherhood and in the man's fatherhood. Human parenthood is something shared by both the man and the woman. Even if the woman, out of love for her husband, says: 'I have given you a child,' her words also mean: 'This is our child.' Although both of them together are parents of their child, *the woman's motherhood constitutes a special 'part' in this shared parenthood*, and the most demanding part. Parenthood – even though it belongs to both – is realized much more fully in the woman, especially in the prenatal period. It is the woman who 'pays' directly for this shared generation, which literally absorbs her energies of her body and soul. It is therefore that *the man* be fully aware that in their shared parenthood he owes *a special debt to the woman*. No program of 'equal rights' between women and men is valid unless it takes this fact fully into account" (*Mulieris Dignitatem*). Pope John Paul II is a hero to mothers! He beautifully acknowledges what it means for a woman to give her body to God and to her husband to be used to bring life into this world. He so chivalrously makes us aware of the extent of the wear and tear on a mother's body and spirit as she unselfishly gives herself to new life.

Isn't it wonderful that our Church has always upheld the dignity of women and motherhood? We should feel peace in our hearts knowing that the gift of our vocation of motherhood is recognized fully for its beauty by our Church – with all its joys, challenges, sacrifices, and sorrows.

1. Why does a mother's love for humanity increase when she becomes a mother?

_____

_____

_____

_____

_____

2. How does a mother lay the foundation for her child's personality?

_____

_____

_____

_____

_____

3. How can children help with their parents' sanctification?

_____

_____

_____

_____

_____

4. How is parenthood realized more fully in the mother?

_____

_____

_____

_____

_____

_____

_____

_____

5. What can I personally do to recognize more fully the immense and holy duties I have as a mother to my children?

_____

_____

_____

_____

_____

_____

_____

_____

Summing Up

We have been discussing the gifts of the souls of our children who are entrusted to us to raise with love and care. We have learned that being open to the gift of life is our "human and Christian responsibility." God the Father has told us, "Be fruitful and multiply, and fill the earth and subdue it." We have read affirmations of our Church's support for our motherhood.

We discussed conception and contraception. We know that our world does not support us in our motherhood and conversely encourages us to put our own selves first and not accept the gift of new life. We should know that the negative connotations about new life that we hear from the culture certainly do not come from God, but rather from the prince of darkness who seeks to drag us to hell with him. We read the warning in Galatians 5:19-21 about the consequences of using contraception. We learned about the approved methods of our Church for spacing our children.

We discussed a mother's "special communion with the mystery of life" and the extraordinary role that mothers have been given. For all of the challenges, sacrifice, and sometimes sorrow that are required in motherhood, it is truly a vocation of indescribable joy.

Thoughts to Ponder

"The history of every human being passes through the threshold of a woman's motherhood; crossing it conditions 'the revelation of the children of God'" *(Mulieris Dignitatem* VI, 19; cf. Rom 8:19).

Even though our culture makes it very difficult at times for a mother to feel encouraged in her vocation, Catholic mothers should take heart and be firmly convinced that our holy Church encourages us, and Our Lord himself does as well. Our Lord actually allows us to form a partnership with him to create human life!

We can find deep joy amid the challenges and fatigue of motherhood, knowing that Our Lord is pleased that we have brought our little ones into the world to raise them up to him, for he has told us, "Let the children come to me, and do not prevent them; for the kingdom of heaven belongs to such as these" (Mt 19:14).

Dear Lord,

Thank you for the amazing blessing of the little souls that fill my life. Thank you for that very special communion with the mystery of life! Help me to always be open to the gift of life and your holy will for my family. With the help of your grace, I pray to be a shining example to others, helping to light the way to heaven in my vocation as a mother.

Amen.

Prayer

4. The Living Room:
In the Heart of the Home

"Let us not grow tired of

doing good, for in due time we

shall reap our harvest,

if we do not give up. So then,

while we have the opportunity,

let us do good to all, but

especially to those who belong

to the family of the faith."

~ Gal 6:9-10

PART ONE CARE OF THE HEARTH: DOMESTIC HAPPINESS

"This is our gift as women.
We have been created to be the center and the heart of the family."

– Blessed Teresa of Calcutta

There's no doubt that the care of the household is a never-ending task. Even when a married couple decides to split some of the household duties, we know that the bulk of the responsibility for the home and children rests fully on the mother's shoulders. Our Lord has given the woman the gift of carrying her baby within her womb and of giving birth. Her role with her children is in an immediate and hands-on way. Children naturally turn to their mother for their countless and varied needs.

Not to slight the father at all of his significant place in the family, but the mother indeed holds a central position in the home. She is the *heart of her home* when she is lovingly dedicating herself to her family. She is a continuous source of love, comfort, and care for her family – someone whose shoes cannot easily be filled.

A mother finds that it is essential to find a proper balance in the way in which she operates the logistics in her home. While she may strive or even just hope to keep perfect order and harmony within her household, she also recognizes the need for flexibility in her schedule keeping according to the unique needs of her children. She realizes that rigidity does not work well at all when caring for her household because she is also dealing with human beings. "To-do" lists may not be checked off in the manner in which she hopes because she is busy caring for the children who depend on her for help, nurturing, and guidance. Many of their needs often require immediate addressing. The children's needs have to take precedence over other matters. Our Lord sees the many selfless acts of loving service performed by the mother in the home. All of the seemingly unimportant or mundane tasks are actually the "holy glue" that keeps the family unit together and moving in the right direction!

"It is not how much we do that is pleasing to God, but how much love we put into the doing. That is what the good God looks for – because he is love and he has made us in his image to love and be loved," Blessed Mother Teresa has told us. She also reminded us that, "We can do no great things – only small things with great love."

We mothers know that our lives are filled with all of those little things in the care of our children: bringing our child a drink of water in the night, soothing our fussy baby, late night infant feedings, bringing peace to bickering siblings, teaching good values, helping with homework – the list is endless, as we well know. However, these are the sometimes unnoticed, everyday tasks of a mom that are so critical to the well-being of her children. When these tasks are performed with love, Our Lord is very pleased. After all, he is the one responsible for putting the mother in the heart of the household to care for her family. So, he knows what we are all about. He's not up there, tapping his foot, expecting the mother to drop to her knees for formal prayer continuously when she is needed in the care of the children.

St Thérèse of Lisieux, the saint of the "Little Way," has taught us to recognize the holiness and sublimity found in little things. "Little" things were also discussed by the late Catholic theologian, Archbishop Fulton J. Sheen, who said, "Our lives for the most part are made up of little things, and by these our character is to be tested…. Little duties carefully discharged; little temptations earnestly resisted with the strength God supplies; little sins crucified; these all together help to form that character which is to be described not as popular or glamorous, but as moral and noble."

Yes, even in doing the menial or not so favored work in the home, we can truly serve Our Lord. I believe it is mostly within those "little" things that we really "earn" our graces! Blessed Teresa of Calcutta told the story about when she visited one of the Missionaries of Charity convents. She came out of the bathroom with a wide smile on her face. She was asked why she was so happy – what had just happened. She replied, "Some Sister here really loves Jesus! The bathroom is sparkling clean!" She was referring to the fact that in wanting to serve Jesus wholeheartedly, we all should want to do our tasks perfectly to please him. Let's try to keep Mother Teresa's smile in mind the next time we face a messy, challenging, or menial task at home!

Family Togetherness

Bringing the family together is largely the mother's doing. She generally prepares and cooks the meals and is the schedule keeper. It's important for mothers to encourage and insist upon the family's presence at the dinner table. But we have to face the fact that today's extremely hectic pace leaves very little time for family togetherness. What's more, we don't have a lot of time when we are actually together. Fathers are usually going off to work in the morning and the kids to school. We usually have one meal at the end of the day where we can come together and be a family. However, even at this time, too many things and issues constantly pull at our attention:

the Internet, homework, phone calls, television, sports practices, activities, meetings, and more.

I've always tried to keep these activities to a dull roar so as not to allow them to overtake our family time, which I feel is *sacred* time. I believe that the family truly is a blessed group of people living together by God's grace to work out their salvation. So doesn't it make sense that our meals together are sacred times? Let's be sure that the busyness prevalent in our day doesn't control our families. We need to make the time for a peaceful occasion at dinner to gather together to pray, communicate, and eat – nourishing our bodies and our souls while resting in Our Lord's peace.

It's up to the moms to foster this practice and make sure that family dinners do indeed take place on a regular basis, where Our Lord will join us. This is not to say that every meal together will be Norman Rockwell picture-perfect, peaceful, and relaxing. Far from it in most households! There will be spills, occasional fighting or crankiness

I believe that the family truly is a blessed group of people living together by God's grace to work out their salvation.... We need to make the time for a peaceful occasion at dinner to gather together to pray, communicate, and eat – nourishing our bodies and our souls while resting in Our Lord's peace.

among the children, or possibly someone in a bad mood for no apparent reason. We deal with it all as it happens. We correct the misbehavior when present, and we strive to converse and include everyone in the conversation. Everything can become a teachable moment. It's a mom's job, though, to strive to make family mealtime nourishing to the body and souls, and also – very importantly – an opportunity for connection with one another as a family. This requires meal planning so we don't find ourselves always at the last minute throwing something together for dinner. If we consider the family meal a blessed time together, we will also view our role in making a nourishing dinner a priority for the family. Naturally, we should not be expected to be "Wonder Woman," and if our day is crazy-busy with the care of the household and children, or illness is thrown into the picture, we make do with macaroni and cheese and salad or sandwiches. Of course, there are households where dad enjoys helping with dinner too, or at least is present at the table to help with the family dynamics and atmosphere to ensure an enjoyable time together as much as possible. Let's also try to keep everyone at the dinner table a few extra moments to enjoy our time together before everyone runs off to do their own thing.

Temptations to Abandon the Heart of the Home

Let's be honest. The noteworthy work of a mother in the home is ironically sometimes – and, even more accurately, most times – unrecognized, unacknowledged, and unappreciated. Moreover, I don't think we'll have any argument from any mother about the fact that the work in the home is often backbreaking, repetitive, and never-ending. The psychological and physical weight of it can loom over a mother with a tremendous pressure. It is not uncommon for a mother to feel discouraged or worn out at times – mostly because she sees no end to the work and doesn't often feel any expression of appreciation for all that she selflessly does.

A mother who is fighting this interior battle may feel, or even state, that she is "just" a mother. I have heard this so often, and I will tell the mom that she is "not *just* a mother!" There are a couple of areas in which a weary or misdirected mother may seek refuge. Since our society is forever suggesting that a woman is only as valuable as her paycheck, this may cause a mom who has dedicated her days to the care of the family to feel unimportant, since she has nothing monetary to show for her hard work. This, coupled with the fact that motherhood is sometimes not appreciated even within her own home, may cause a mother to seek outside employment to satisfy her feelings of insecurity or possibly even resentment.

If there is not a financial need for the mother to work outside the home, she should dedicate herself to the care of her children and withhold working outside the home until her children are at least six or seven years old, and then only do so when safe and loving arrangements for the children are provided while she is away. Additionally, it's important for the mother to arrange her schedule so that she can be home when her children arrive home from school to greet them and care for them. This is also true in the case of homeschooling situations; the mother should arrange her employment hours so that her teaching time is completed and a relative or competent and loving caregiver is in place. Otherwise, others who may not hold the mother's values are raising her children. Additionally, the mother and children miss out on their precious and essential time together.

Some may argue that a mother should not feel "chained" to her household and that she would feel better if she had time away. I am not suggesting that a mother should feel like a slave to her housework and care of her children; however, I am attempting to point out the importance of a mother dedicating her life to rearing her children so that she will truly be answering God's request for her vocation. Any time that a mother deserts her children's care, she is opening wide the door to possible chaos and instability, and again – other people's values and morals – or the lack thereof – are thrust upon the innocent and impressionable children.

Lest you think I am a "slave-driver" or an uncaring person, of course I know that mothers are very deserving of a break from their work in the home. Certainly this should be organized with the help of her husband so that she will not be unnecessarily overworked. Her tireless efforts and labors should be acknowledged and appreciated. Mothers should teach their children to express their appreciation often. A mother cares for her family because she loves them, but she teaches her children not to take her for granted and to also help out when they are of an appropriate age.

Another area that may threaten a mother's time in her household is having too much participation in outside activities, as I previously mentioned, however wholesome or holy they may seem. If a mother gets involved in too many committees and activities outside of the home, she may inadvertently neglect her family's needs. She should be very careful in this regard. This is not to say that she cannot work out a mutually convenient schedule whereby the father, grandmother, or other relative helps out within the home in the care of the children and household so that the mother can partake in some worthwhile pursuits. She can also trade off times with a close like-minded friend or relative to achieve her desires to help others. Recourse to prayer and deep reflection is a certain antidote to this potential problem.

It's crucial to keep an eye on all of this and prayerfully discern what would work out best for the family as a whole. Motherhood is filled with sacrifice, as we know, and one particular sacrifice is in putting one's own desires on hold for the betterment of the family. The children grow up very quickly, and it is important that we will be present to them in all of their needs and most especially while they are young.

1. Why is the mother called to take her place at the heart of the home?

_____

_____

_____

_____

_____

_____

_____

_____

2. Why is God pleased with a mother's acts of loving service within her household?

_____

_____

_____

_____

_____

_____

_____

_____

3. Why should a mother hold off from working outside of the home if this is possible?

_____

_____

_____

_____

_____

_____

_____

4. What is one way to figure out what a mother should do regarding outside employment?

_____

_____

_____

_____

_____

_____

_____

_____

PART TWO EVERYDAY HOLINESS: FIRST AND
FOREMOST EDUCATOR

"The fecundity of conjugal love cannot be reduced to the
procreation of children, but must extend to their moral education
and their spiritual formation. 'The role of parents in
education is of such importance that it is almost impossible
to provide an adequate substitute.' The right and duty of parents to
educate their children are primordial and inalienable."

– The Catechism of the Catholic Church, 2221

One of the most important roles of a mother is of being the first and foremost educator to her children. One of the documents of the Second Vatican Council speaks about our grave responsibility in the education of our children and says, "Scarcely anything can compensate for their failure in it." We read, "Since parents have conferred life on their children, they have a most solemn obligation to educate their offspring. Hence, parents must be acknowledged as the first and foremost educators of their children. Their role as educators is so decisive that scarcely anything can compensate for their failure in it. For it devolves on parents to create a family atmosphere so animated with love and reverence for God and others that a well-rounded personal and social development will be fostered among children. Hence, the family is the first school of those social virtues which every society needs" (*Gravissimum Educationis*). These words should comfort and encourage our mother's hearts as well as reinforce our dedication in our teaching role with our children. We are provided with strong and profound words to ponder!

We are consistently encouraged and instructed by Mother Church. Pope John Paul II recalled the words above from *Gravissimum Educationis* in his apostolic exhortation, *Familiaris Consortio*. He further instructed, "The task of giving education is rooted in the primary vocation of married couples to participate in God's creative activity: by begetting in love and for love a new person who has within himself or herself the vocation to growth and development, parents by that very fact take on the task of helping that person effectively to live a fully human life."

Catholic mothers are passionately urged by our Church to make it their duty and mission, while considering it their privilege, to educate their children in faith and truth. Our Lord does not ask us to bring our children into this world and then become lackadaisical about their education. As a matter of fact, the Catechism states that, "The fecundity of conjugal love cannot be reduced solely to procreation of children, but must extend to their moral education and their spiritual formation. 'The *role of parents in education* is of such importance that it is almost impossible to provide an adequate substitute.' The right and duty of parents to educate their children are primordial and inalienable" (CCC, 2221; *Familiaris Consortio*, 36).

Pope John Paul II also instructed us, "The right and duty of parents to give education is essential, since it is connected with the transmission of human life; it is *original and primary* with regard to the educational role of others, on account of the uniqueness of the loving relationship between parents and children; and it is *irreplaceable and inalienable*, and therefore incapable of being entirely delegated to others or usurped by others. In addition to these characteristics, it cannot be forgotten that the most basic element, so basic that it qualifies the educational role of parents, is *parental love*, which finds fulfillment in the task of education as it completes and perfects its service of life: as well as being a *source*, the parents' love is also the *animating principle* and therefore the *norm* inspiring and guiding all concrete educational activity, enriching it with the values of kindness, constancy, goodness, service, disinterestedness, and self-sacrifice that are the most precious fruit of love."

We are also reminded by Pope Benedict XVI of the vital task in our role as first educator and of the fact that our homes become our children's first schools and our domestic churches. He said, "As the first school of life and of faith, and as a 'domestic church,' the family is called to educate new generations in human and Christian values so as to forge in them – guiding their lives according to the model of Christ – a well-balanced personality. In such a vital task...it is important to have the support of the school, of the parish, and of the various ecclesial groups that favor the integral education of human beings" (from a letter written to Cardinal Alfonso Lopez Trujillo, president of the Pontifical Council for the Family, Oct. 2007).

Mothers should not expect others to fully educate their children. While of course other teachers will fill their children's lives, parents are the first and foremost educators. It is a parent's duty to be sure that their children are taught the truth about God and the Church and to counteract any wrong teaching that their children may come in contact with through their schools, the culture, or their religious education.

Our homes become our children's first schools and our domestic churches.... The family is called to educate new generations in human and Christian values so as to forge in them – guiding their lives according to the model of Christ – a well-balanced personality.

Recognizing Our Lord within Our Domestic Church

One thing we know for sure – mothers cannot possibly fail to recognize the unending tasks that call for her attention and that may even loom over her in her household. These are the ones that are right in her face, beckoning for her immediate response: children's pressing needs, hampers overflowing with soiled clothes, dirty dishes in the sink, and "dust bunnies" that seem to mock her! She often writes her "to-do" list in her mind or on paper in the evenings, consisting of the many jobs in her home that she hopes to accomplish the following day, phone calls to set up appointments, errands to run, and supplies needed for the household. She then remains "on call" to her family's needs throughout the night.

By outward appearances, it could seem as though diapers, demands, laundry, and dishes are the only activities filling her days and nights. With so much to do in the limited hours of a day, a mother may begin to feel frustrated and dwell on what she may perceive as her lack of accomplishments. She may also fail to see Our Lord's hand mystically in all of this.

Our Lord is very much aware of the extent of a mother's busyness in her dedication to her work in the home and family – he has given her the sublime privilege of raising little saints up to heaven right within the walls of her home! However, because mothers are inundated with this care of their families, they may fail to recognize that Our Lord is also living under their roofs assisting them all along the way.

Pope John Paul II referred to the home very often as a "domestic church." He also has asked us to model ourselves after the Holy Family of Nazareth. He said, "For every believer, and especially for Christian families, the humble dwelling place in Nazareth is *an authentic school of the Gospel.* Here we admire, put into practice, the divine plan to make the family an *intimate community of life and love;* here we learn that every Christian family is called to be a small *'domestic church'* that must shine with the Gospel virtues. Recollection and prayer, mutual understanding and respect, personal discipline and community asceticism, and a spirit of sacrifice, work, and solidarity are typical features that make the family of Nazareth a model for every home" (Pope John Paul II, Feast of the Holy Family, Sunday, December 30, 2001).

We read in the Catechism, "The Christian family constitutes a specific revelation and realization of ecclesial communion, and for this reason it can be and should be called a *domestic church.* It is a community of faith, hope, and charity; it assumes singular importance in the Church, as is evident in the New Testament" (CCC, 2204).

I think it's great that we have a "domestic church" right within the walls of our homes. Blessed Mother Teresa, whom I had the privilege to know, often referred to the domestic church as well. She regularly preached that our love must begin at home. By recognizing this fact, we can strive to emulate what Pope John Paul II mentioned above so that our church of the home "shines with Gospel values." He calls us to "recollection and prayer, mutual understanding and respect, personal discipline and community asceticism and a spirit of sacrifice, work, and solidarity." Is this what exudes within and from our households? Are we teaching our children these values? We must ask ourselves these questions. We should be sure to put up images of Our Lord, the Blessed Mother, and the saints around our *domestic churches*. Crucifixes hanging in each bedroom are also important. I actually have the crucifix that was on my bedroom wall as a child above my bed now, a bit broken and all. I like to have rosary beads all around the house too. All of these holy images will make an impression on our children and even on us.

Many times, I want to be in front of the Blessed Sacrament, alone with Jesus so that I can pour my heart out to him and seek his comfort, grace, and love; instead, I am caring for family situations in the household: sick children or an emergency that crops up. Other times, I crave the thought of extra daily Masses and public devotions in which to participate alone or with my brood. Responsibilities with the family, a debilitating migraine headache, or other infirmities at times will get in the way of me leaving my house. Other times, a friend or neighbor may call on the telephone or show up at the door with a serious situation on their hands that requires assistance immediately. Charity comes before my desire to be at Church. At these times, I need to take comfort and be content in my *domestic church* where my prayers are voiced through my loving actions.

Our Lord knows what's going on. We must turn our homes into little churches and live lives of holiness, offering our daily duties to Our Lord with love, knowing that he is in control. We cannot always run off to the building of the Church to seek him, rather we must find him within our homes, family members, and neighbors. Of course we fulfill our obligations for weekly Mass and holy days, yet even in these, if a child is sick and we need to care for him or her – our duty is there with our child.

We can also read in Ephesians 5:21–6:4 to learn about the responsibility of being subject to one another in the family unit of our domestic churches. Pope John Paul II also addressed this subjectivity in *The Theology of Marriage and Celibacy*. He said,

"The opening expression of our passage of Ephesians 5:21-23, which we have approached by an analysis of the remote and immediate context, has quite a special eloquence. The author speaks of the mutual subjection of the spouses, husband and wife, and in this way he explains the words which he will unite afterwards on the subjection of the spouses, husband and wife. In fact, we read: 'Wives be subject to your husbands, as to the Lord' (5:22). In saying this, the author does not intend to say that the husband is the 'lord' of the wife and that the interpersonal pact proper to marriage is a pact of domination of the husband over the wife. Instead, he expresses a different concept: that is, that the wife can and should find in her relationship with Christ, who is the one Lord of both the spouses – the motivation of that relationship with her husband which flows from the very essence of marriage and of the family. Such a relationship, however, is not one of one-sided domination. Marriage, according to the letter to the Ephesians, excludes the element of the pact, which was a burden and, at times, does not cease to be a burden on this institution. The husband and the wife are in fact 'subject to one another' and are mutually subordinated to one another. The source of this mutual subjection is to be found in Christian pietas, and its expression is love.

"Love excludes every kind of subjection whereby the wife might become a servant or a slave of the husband, an object of unilateral domination. Love makes the husband simultaneously subject to the wife, and thereby subject to the Lord himself, just as the wife to the husband. The community or unity, which they should establish through marriage, is constituted by a reciprocal donation of self, which is also a mutual subjection. Christ is the source and at the same time the model of that subjection, which being reciprocal 'out of reverence for Christ,' confers on the conjugal union a profound and mature character." We are called to be subject to and in service to one another in our families. This will be indeed where we work out our holiness.

Again, in *Mulieris Dignitatem*, Pope John Paul II addressed that subject of mutual giving of self. He said, "The author of the Letter to the Ephesians sees no contradiction between an exhortation formulated in this way and the words: 'Wives, be subject to your husbands, as to the Lord; for the husband is head of the wife' (5:22-23). The author knows that this way of speaking, so profoundly rooted in the customs and religious traditions of the time, is to be understood and carried out in a new way: as a *'mutual subjection out of reverence for Christ'* (cf. Eph 5:21).

This is especially true because the husband is called the 'head' of the wife *as* Christ is the head of the Church; he is so in order to give 'himself up for her' (Eph 5:25), and giving himself up for her means giving up his own life. However, whereas in the relationship between Christ and the Church the subjection is only on the part of the Church, in the relationship between husband and wife the 'subjection' is not one-sided but mutual" (*MD* VI, 24).

Mothers can prayerfully offer their days to the Lord, asking for his graces and blessings to be bestowed upon her family as she – being the very heart of the home – helps them to work out their salvation by her word and example through her selfless role within the walls of her home. Once a Christian mother recognizes Our Lord dwelling within her household, she will have peace of heart knowing that the endless and sometimes monotonous tasks are not at all unimportant and ordinary – rather, they are the extraordinary works of love that please Our Lord very much. By offering her days to the Lord in prayer, a mother helps to sanctify her actions within the *domestic church*.

1. *How is the task of giving education to your children connected with the transmission of life?*

_____

_____

_____

_____

_____

_____

_____

2. *What is at the root of the educational role of parents and drives them to educate their children?*

_____

_____

_____

_____

_____

_____

_____

_____

_____

3. *What are some ways that you can make your home a* domestic church?

_____

_____

_____

_____

_____

_____

4. *How can a mother see Our Lord's hand in her everyday role in the home?*

_____

_____

_____

_____

_____

5. *How can a mother sanctify her day?*

_____

_____

_____

_____

_____

Summing Up

We have discussed many aspects of the heart of the home – the precise place where a Christian mother finds her purpose and grows in holiness. We talked about the sometimes monotonous and unrecognized tasks in the home that a mother performs with love for her family. Many of the saints, including St Thérèse of Lisieux and Blessed Teresa of Calcutta, have taught us about the sublimity within simplicity and in doing "little" things with great love.

Mothers, as we know, have a difficult job in the home coupled with the fact that society oftentimes demeans the role of a mother by "measuring" her worth by the size of her paycheck. There are areas that a mother may try to "escape" to in order to feel more accomplished while inadvertently neglecting her family.

We discussed that mothers are enlightened by our Church to make it their duty and mission, while considering it their privilege to educate their children in faith and truth and that they cannot expect others to fulfill that responsibility.

Diapers, demands, laundry, and dishes are not the only activities filling a mother's time. However, a mother may begin to feel frustrated and dwell on what she feels is her lack of accomplishments. She may also fail to see Our Lord's hand in her housekeeping because of the mixed messages from our society aimed at mothers and also because she may be exhausted and in need of encouragement. Mothers should strive to help one another with Christian camaraderie and encouragement for the journey.

Blessed Mother Teresa reminds us, "Mothers are the heart of the home; they build family life by wanting, loving, and taking care of their children. Mothers make the home a center of love. Their role is sometimes hard, but there is the example of the Blessed Virgin, who teaches us to be good with our children."

Thoughts to Ponder

What a privilege it is to hold a central position in the home! A mother is the heart of her home when she is lovingly dedicating herself to her family. In her role as a continuous source of love, comfort, and care for her family, she will actually work out her salvation and help with her family's salvation, as well. What a beautiful gift that or Lord has bestowed upon mothers! When a Christian mother comes to realize that it is in serving others within her domestic church that she will *find* herself, she will experience a deep joy and peace of heart undoubtedly incomparable to anything else imaginable.

We are reminded in the Catechism that "The Christian family constitutes a specific revelation and realization of ecclesial communion, and for this reason it can be and should be called a *domestic church*. It is a community of faith, hope, and charity; it assumes singular importance in the Church, as is evident in the New Testament" (CCC, 2204).

Prayer

Dear Lord,

Please open my eyes to see you within my domestic church. Please give me peace in my vocation as mother where I strive for holiness within my household, working out my salvation and my family's. Thank you for this awesome privilege! Help me not to squander these blessings and graces, but rather offer everything to you so that it can all be sanctified.

Amen.

5. The Kitchen:
A Vocation of Love

"We have known and
believe the love that God
has for us. God is love, and
those who abide in
love abide in God, and God
abides in them."

~ 1 Jn 4:16

PART ONE A LOVE THAT COMPELS US

"Charity is the soul of the holiness to which all are called: it governs, shapes, and perfects all the means of sanctification."

– Lumen Gentium, 42

Pondering what the Apostle John teaches about love, we can read in the Gospel of John, "We have known and believe the love that God has for us. God is love, and those who abide in love abide in God, and God abides in them. Love has been perfected among us in this: that we may have boldness on the day of judgment, because as he is so are we in this world. There is no fear in love, but perfect love casts out all fear; for fear has to do with punishment, and whoever fears has not reached perfection in love. We love because he first loved us. Those who say, 'I love God,' and hate their brother or sister are liars; for those who do not love a brother or sister whom they have seen, cannot love God whom they have not seen. The commandment we have from him is this: those who love God must love their brothers and sisters also" (1 Jn 4:16-21). Our Lord has always called us to live lives of love.

Pope Benedict XVI used St. John's words to open his first encyclical, *Deus Caritas Est*. He wrote, "These words from the First Letter of John express with remarkable clarity the heart of the Christian faith: the Christian image of God and the resulting image of mankind and its destiny. In the same verse, St. John also offers a kind of summary of the Christian life: 'We have come to know and to believe in the love God has for us.'"

Motherhood is certainly a vocation filled with love. A prayerful mother will come to know and to believe in the love God has for her so that she can truly pass that love on to her family. Mothers encounter God and his love each and every day in the midst of their families. He is there in their homes, their laundry rooms, at their kitchen tables, and truly living within every aspect of their domestic churches.

"Charity must not remain hidden in the bottom of the heart," St. Thérèse of Lisieux has told us. For mothers, charity couldn't possibly remain hidden, for love is indubitably worn on a mother's sleeves. It is what a mother's life is all about – it's actually the fabric of her life. Love is what compels mothers to do all that they do for their families. A mother's vocation is to love her family and through that dedicated love, to work out her own salvation while she is guiding her family to work out theirs as well.

Blessed Teresa of Calcutta reminds us that "Love begins at home; love lives in homes." If we are to correct problems and the lack of love in our society, and "if we are to bring that love into life again," she said, "we have to begin at home." Wouldn't it be wonderful if our world would understand? Yet, rather than become frustrated with its lack of comprehension, we can strive to be a radiant example of love which can change the world, family by family.

When it comes to loving our babies and children, the good Lord has given mothers a wonderful bonding chemical messenger called oxytocin, plus other messengers and hormones: prolactin, opioids, norepinephrine, and pheromones. During pregnancies and mothering, these God-given ingredients all play a part in helping mothers to establish the proper responses for their unborn babies, their infants and children – to follow their maternal cues to nurture their offspring with tender love, frequent touch, cuddling, and feedings.

During the birth process, oxytocin is at work, furthering the bonding between mother and child

"Love begins at home; love lives in homes." If we are to correct problems and the lack of love in our society, and "if we are to bring that love into life again, we have to begin at home."

and helping to relax the two of them. The amazing and beneficial hormone prolactin is released during the suckling of the infant and promotes care-giving behaviors for the mother, in addition to allowing for more relaxation.

For adoptive mothers, feeding their babies with tenderness while holding them (rather than propping a bottle) also increases levels of oxytocin in mother and baby which helps the mother to be more caring, eager to please, more sensitive to others feelings, able to recognize nonverbal cues more readily, while it also helps both mother and baby to be more relaxed and content. Our Lord has it all figured out!

Once a woman learns that she is pregnant, she becomes very aware that there is a little person who depends on her for its life. This reality alone greatly changes a woman, compelling her to take on the full attitude of a mother. She is no longer just a woman or a wife – she has become a mother who has been given the awesome responsibility to keep her child safe and thriving to the very best of her ability. She will be the one whose decisions and actions affect that child for better or for worse in the most direct way. This is the moment when a woman's own interests and desires will be put on hold for the sake of dedicating herself more fully to her child. Her thoughts are no longer for herself alone and for her husband, but for another person who has come into their lives. The love in her maternal heart grows with each child that Our Lord will bless her with.

I have always been impressed with Blessed Teresa of Calcutta's sentiments about how love truly begins at home. She said, "Make your house, your family, another Nazareth where love, peace, joy, and unity reign, for love begins at home. You must start there and make your home the center of burning love. You must be the hope of eternal happiness to your wife, your husband, your child, to your grandfather, grandmother, to whoever is connected with you."

If we can't find love at home, where can we expect to find it? It must begin right in our hearts and flourish in our homes to affect all of our family members and beyond.

1. *Read 1 Jn 4:16-21. How does love cast out all fear? Can you think of times in your life when you were fearful during a certain situation and how the love of a parent, spouse, relative, friend, or religious helped you? Have you had recourse to Our Lord in prayer when you were fearful? If so, has that helped you in alleviating your fear about that situation you faced?*

_____

_____

_____

_____

_____

_____

2. *What does Pope Benedict consider to be the heart of the Christian faith? And why do you think this is?*

_____

_____

_____

_____

_____

3. *Why do you think love should begin at home, and what does that really mean?*

---

4. *What can you do to ensure that love is really at the heart of your home?*

PART TWO A LOVE THAT CHALLENGES US

"Without love there is no true life in the family. Even if it passes

through various difficulties, lacking things, or suffering,

if love remains, the family will remain solid and united."

– Pope John Paul II, May 1, 1989

Pope John Paul II told us in *Mulieris Dignitatem*, "The eternal mystery of generation, which is in God himself, the one and triune God (cf. Eph 3:14-15), is reflected in the woman's motherhood and in the man's fatherhood. Human parenthood is something shared by both the man and the woman. Even if the woman, out of love for her husband, says: 'I have given you a child,' her words also mean: 'This is our child.' Although both of them together are parents of their child, *the woman's motherhood constitutes a special 'part' in this shared parenthood*, and the most demanding part. Parenthood – even though it belongs to both – is realized much more fully in the woman, especially in the prenatal period. It is the woman who 'pays' directly for this shared generation, which literally absorbs the energies of her body and soul. It is therefore necessary that *the man* be fully aware that in their shared parenthood he owes *a special debt to the woman*. No program of 'equal rights' between women and men is valid unless it takes this fully into account."

These words should comfort us mothers, knowing that our Church recognizes the sacrifices and demands of true Christian motherhood which literally absorb "the energies of her body and soul." The love that a mother is called to is very challenging. It calls us to put everything else aside and do all in our power – exerting all of our energies to nurture and love the blessings of the souls that have been entrusted to us. It calls us to give up our own bodies to house the infants who grow within us – their first environment – changing our shape, at times causing some discomfort, morning sickness, or sacrifice, while they poke around in us, their little feet up in our rib cages during some of our sleepless nights. This love calls us to think and feel for someone else, drawing us up out of our own needs and wants.

At times a mother's love is like a healing balm to her family. A mother, being a source of comfort and love, helps to ease the occasional tension or discord throughout the daily life of the family that may sometimes be present due to clashing of personalities and growing pains. A mother is the peacemaker, bringing calmness to squabbling siblings. She sometimes waits quietly and patiently for her husband to come to recognize her points in a discussion rather than becoming unbearably pushy about her position, knowing that the former approach will be more effective for everyone. There will also be times when, for the sake of family, the mother will need to be very outspoken, not compromising one bit, exercising her use of authority in her role as the heart of the home as she guides her children because a mother knows that she would rather be loving and firm in her expectations for her children than to be popular so that they will be safe and headed in the right direction.

St. Thomas Aquinas said, "To love is to will the good of another" (*Summa Theologiae*, I-II). As her children grow, there will be times when a mother's expectations and rules may not be very well liked by her adolescent and teenaged children as I mentioned earlier. Mothers are challenged in their vocation to truly love with a love so deep that it is sacrificial – by giving of herself for the good of another. Sometimes love means laying down the law and the parameters for their children to keep them safe in every way. Our children require our authority over them and absolutely need us to set very clear boundaries so that there will not be any confusion as to what is expected of them. We know that when we must correct and discipline our children in love, they may not be very happy with us for a time. Our love for them challenges us to do what is right and holy for their sakes, putting our wants or needs for love from them in return aside for the time being.

Disciplining our children may take various approaches, depending on unique situations. A single mother I knew shared an experience with me about her teenage daughter. Her daughter was not seeing eye to eye with her and decided to run away for a couple of days. This shenanigan just about broke her mother's heart. She had no idea where she could possibly have gone wrong in raising her daughter. She always prayed to be a very good mother, and I knew that she was very loving to her children because it was always obvious in all of their interactions.

This mother went to her parish priest who was known for his sometimes "fire and brimstone" homilies. She told me that she knew him well and could trust him for sound advice. This faithful mother had absolutely no idea what to do and wanted to handle the whole distressing situation in the way that Our Lord wanted her to. She knew that she had to come up with the proper consequences for her daughter for doing such a crazy and scary thing.

The counsel she received from the priest was far from what she had expected. "Make a nice dinner for her, and welcome her home with open arms. Don't say anything about what happened," he told her. She was to treat her daughter like the prodigal son. This mother was flabbergasted with this counsel! However, she could see and understand the wisdom in it. She followed the holy advice exactly, and she told me that she felt her daughter was overcome by the love shown to her when she came back home that evening without the persecution of the "third degree." The mother found a more appropriate time a few days later when things were calm to discuss the issue with her daughter. Her daughter was very thankful for a happy homecoming, and the continued understanding and love grew between them over time.

Blessed Teresa of Calcutta, I believe, set the record straight regarding the origin of the discord in the world. She said, "Everybody today seems to be in such a terrible rush, anxious for greater developments and greater riches and so on, so that children have very little time for their parents. Parents have very little time for each other, and in the home begins the disruption of the peace of the world." Perhaps we can keep this in mind as we plan our days and our lives so that we can be sure to have family time together on a regular basis.

"Everybody today seems to be in such a terrible rush, anxious for greater developments and greater riches and so on, so that children have very little time for their parents. Parents have very little time for each other, and in the home begins the disruption of the peace of the world."

1. *What are some ways that love challenges mothers?*

_____

_____

_____

_____

_____

_____

_____

_____

_____

2. *Do you think the Church understands the fullness of the*
demands on a mother to raise her children?

_____

_____

_____

_____

_____

_____

3 . What are the times that a mother's love becomes sacrificial?

_____

_____

_____

_____

_____

_____

_____

_____

_____

4. What can mothers do to love with Jesus' love?

_____

_____

_____

_____

_____

_____

_____

Summing Up

We have discussed a mother's vocation of love: natural, compelling and challenging. A mother, being truly the heart of the home in her vocation of love, lives a life of active faith, hope, and love, calling her family to holiness and sanctification. When a mother is challenged in her vocation of love she should go to prayer often, seeking grace and strength to fulfill her duties. We are reminded in *Lumen Gentium* that "Charity is the soul of the holiness to which all are called: it 'governs, shapes, and perfects all the means of sanctification'" (*LG*, 42). Charity (love) is truly the secret and the answer.

Thoughts to Ponder

In her book, *Story of a Soul*, St. Thérèse said, "If the Church was a body composed of different members, it couldn't lack the noblest of all; *it must have a Heart, and a Heart* **burning with love**. And I realized that this love alone was the true motive force which enabled the other members of the Church to act; if it ceased to function, the Apostles would forget to preach the Gospel; the Martyrs would refuse to shed their blood. *Love, in fact, is the vocation which includes all others; it's a universe of its own comprising all time and space – it's eternal!*"

A mother's role in the home is the "noblest of all," enabling all members of the family to exist, to act, to function, and to grow in love, according to St. Thérèse's thinking. When a mother's heart is "burning with love" her family will know and feel the effects and cannot help but be moved and changed for the better, even when at times it may seem so apparent. Mothers can fuel the fire of love in their hearts for their family through faithful prayer.

PRAYER
Please give me strength and grace

"Love is a fruit in season at all times and within the reach of every hand. Anyone may gather it and no limit is set. Everyone can reach this love through meditation, prayer, sacrifice, and an intense inner life."
– Blessed Teresa of Calcutta

Dear Lord,

Please give me strength and grace in my vocation of love. Help me to grow in faith, hope, and love daily as I guide my family to holiness and sanctification. Please light the fire in my heart so that it will burn with love for you and also so that I may draw others to you with the fire of love in my heart.

Amen.

6. The Dining Room:
Praying in the Domestic Church

"It should never be forgotten
that prayer constitutes an essential
part of the Christian life,
understood in its fullness and
centrality. Indeed, prayer is an
important part of our very humanity;
it is 'the first expression of man's
inner truth, the first condition for
authentic freedom of spirit.'"

~ Pope John Paul II,
Address at the Mentorella Shrine,
October 29, 1978

Part One 〰 Praying Mother: Sanctifying Herself and Her Family

"But those who drink of the water that I will give them will never be thirsty. The water that I will give them will become in them a spring of water gushing up to eternal life."

– Jn 4:14

A Christian mother understands the necessity for prayer in her life – deep prayer for strength and guidance for rearing her family along with her husband within a culture that undermines and contradicts good morality. In 1 Thes 5:18, we are reminded to "give thanks in all circumstances." The Catechism tells us that, "Every joy and suffering, every event and need can become the matter for thanksgiving which, sharing in that of Christ, should fill one's whole life" (CCC, 2648). Consequently, we see that we can make use of the unlimited occasions throughout our lives for giving thanks in prayer; every joy, event, and suffering can become opportunities for prayer. In short, we can transform our daily lives into prayers, even while we are busy mothering – beseeching Our Lord for his grace and blessings, asking for guidance and giving thanks always.

Blessed Teresa of Calcutta said, "We must make our homes centers of compassion and forgive endlessly." This surely is the secret to happiness in our families. We must give, and give with love and forgiveness to know real peace in our hearts and to see God at work in our homes.

Food for the Soul

"Pray constantly…always and for everything giving thanks in the name of Our Lord Jesus Christ to God the Father."

– 1 Thes 5:17; Eph 5:20

Mothers have been entrusted with the care and nurturing of their children. However, equally as important as the food for their children's stomachs is the food for their souls. In order for a mother to form her children in the faith and in prayer, she must be sure to form it within herself first. She must draw closer to God through a deep and constant prayer life.

A mother may struggle to find specific dedicated prayer times throughout her busy days because she is at the service of her children who need her attention. At times, throughout her mothering, she may not have much opportunity to break away from her routine. Since a mother fully realizes that her days are filled to capacity with the care of others, she finds that she should dedicate her entire day to the Lord,

A *mother will undoubtedly grow in holiness as she strives to keep her heart and mind lifted to heaven whenever she is able, while she is going about her duties in the home.*

beginning the first thing in the morning, offering all of her prayers, works, joys, and sufferings and asking that they become a means to her salvation and of her family as well. She then knows that she has offered her Lord *everything* and has asked him to bless it all. She realizes that there might not be many occasions, particularly when her children are very young and requiring a lot of hands-on care, when she can get down on her knees to pray, hence she offers to God all of her many loving acts of service to her family from where she has been called to serve from the heart of her home. A mother will undoubtedly grow in holiness as she strives to keep her heart and mind lifted to heaven whenever she is able, while she is going about her duties in the home. Therefore, a mother strives to find the opportunities for her dedicated prayer time, as well as being sure to dedicate her entire day to the Lord, so that all of her actions will be blessed and a means to her sanctification.

St. John Vianney, Cure of Ars, so beautifully and passionately expressed his love for God in a prayer he wrote: "I love you, O my God, and my only desire is to love you until the last breath of my life. I love you, O my infinitely lovable God, and I would rather die loving you, than live without loving you. I love you, Lord, and the only grace I ask is to love you eternally…. My God, if my tongue cannot say in every moment that I love you, I want my heart to repeat it to you as often as I draw breath." His words give mothers a cause to pause and ponder. Can we also courageously, and with complete trust, offer every beat of our hearts for love of Our Lord? Yes, we can!

Love is the certain source of prayer; whoever draws from it reaches the summit of prayer (cf. CCC, 2658). When a mother's heart is burning with love for her God and her family, she too can ask Our Lord if her every breath can become a prayer of love to him. She can ask if her acts of loving service within her family can be transformed into prayers of love to him.

We learn about a parent's dignity and mission and very specific responsibility to guide their children in the faith from *Familiaris Consortio*: "By reason of their dignity and mission, Christian parents have the specific responsibility of educating their children in prayer, introducing them to a gradual discovery of the mystery of God and to personal dialogue with him: 'It is particularly in the Christian family, enriched by the grace and the office of the sacrament of matrimony, that from the earliest years children should be taught, according to the faith received in baptism, to have a knowledge of God, worship him and love their neighbor.'"

Mothers should call upon the grace from the sacrament of matrimony, which is available for the asking! Our Lord will provide much grace to facilitate the lessons in prayer within the walls of the home. A mother can, and should, pray in her children's presence. She can offer little prayers of aspiration to Our Lord and his Blessed Mother as she feeds her infants and cares for her children. They will learn by her example. As they grow, she teaches them to bless themselves with the Sign of the Cross and encourages them to enter into a dialogue with Jesus and his Blessed Mother. These will be the formative building blocks of prayer instilled in her children's hearts that they will draw upon throughout life.

Three Kinds of Domestic Prayer

Christian mothers have three areas in which to develop prayer: They need to shape a strong prayer life of their own, teach their children to cultivate their own personal prayer lives, and encourage and facilitate family prayer. A mother needs a strong foundation of personal prayer to stand strong at the center of the heart of her home. She should teach her children to pray each day, encouraging them to pray with her as well as on their own. Family prayer is necessary to keep the family unit intact. Blessed Teresa always said, "A family that prays together stays together."

There may be times throughout the tapestry of motherhood when a Christian mother may be required to trust in Our Lord's mercy and his promises while she relates to St. Monica's pleadings in prayer for her wayward son, Augustine. Even when a strong foundation of prayer is laid down in the family, our older children may go astray temporarily, getting sidetracked from the narrow path, searching to find their own way. It is then when we double up on our prayers and sacrifices and trust that Our Lord hears the prayers of a faithful mother and that the words to St. Monica from her bishop regarding her son apply to all mothers: "God will never turn his ear from a woman of all those tears." We should know that the foundation of prayer that we have built for our children will undoubtedly remain with them, holding them up and leaving "an impression that the future events in their lives will not be able to efface," as Pope John Paul II has told us. We must never give up on hope! We must be faithful in prayer for our families always! Our Lord is counting on us. A mother's work for the sanctification of her children is never complete because she prays constantly for them, no matter how old they are, and even into eternity.

1. *Why is it necessary for a mother to have a deep prayer life?*

_____

_____

_____

_____

_____

_____

2. *How can mothers make use of their everyday joys and sufferings to pray?*

_____

_____

_____

_____

_____

_____

3. *What are the ingredients to a happy home life? (Answers will vary.)*

_____

_____

_____

_____

_____

_____

4. *What are the three areas of prayer that a mother should be concerned with?*

_____

_____

_____

_____

_____

_____

_____

5. *How can a mother be successful in finding time for prayer?*

_____

_____

_____

_____

_____

_____

_____

_____

PART TWO ❧ A PRAYING FAMILY: SANCTIFYING THE
ECCLESIAL COMMUNITY AND THE WORLD

"Pray at all times in the Spirit, with all prayer

and supplication. To that end keep alert with all perseverance

making supplication for all the saints."

– Eph 6:18

It's amazing to know that a Christian family is considered to be a
"priestly people which is the Church." Pope John Paul II told us in
Familiaris Consortio, "The Christian family too is part of this priestly
people which is the Church. By means of the sacrament of marriage,
in which it is rooted and from which it draws its nourishment, the
Christian family is continuously vivified by the Lord Jesus and called
and engaged by him in a dialogue with God through the sacraments,
through the offering of one's life, and through prayer.

"This is the *priestly role* which the Christian family can and ought
to exercise in intimate communion with the whole Church, through
the daily realities of married and family life. In this way the Christian
family *is called to be sanctified and to sanctify the ecclesial community
and the world"* (FC IV, 55).

Again, we are reminded of the power and grace within the sacrament of marriage. We are told that because the Christian family is part of the priestly people which is the Church, they are called to engage in dialogue with Our Lord. This conversation of prayer with Our Lord indeed occurs during the daily routine of family life where God has put the mother to work out her salvation – within the ordinariness of her days.

The Catechism tells us, "Prayer in the events of each day and each moment is one of the secrets of the kingdom revealed to 'little children,' to the servants of Christ, to the poor of the Beatitudes. It is right and good to pray so that the coming of the kingdom of justice and peace may influence the march of history, but it is just as important to bring the help of prayer into humble, everyday situations; all forms of prayer can be the leaven to which the Lord compares the kingdom" (CCC, 2660). Our Catechism gives us such a richness of information and insight for Catholic families. It's a book that should be picked up often to reflect upon to nourish our minds, hearts, and souls.

We know that our example to our children speaks volumes and is heard much louder and with more clarity than our words could ever be. Mothers absolutely have to set the example for prayer in the household. Family prayer time needs to be established. Teaching our children to develop their own individual prayer lives is essential and they will learn much of this by observing a praying mother.

There are a few areas where we can easily fit family prayer into our everyday lives. At the family table at meals, prayers can be said together after grace, and also in the morning and evening. Short prayers get the day started on the right foot together, as well as ending the day in each child's bedroom or all together, offering it all to God. At other times, we can plan a set time to gather together as a family community for a decade of the rosary on a Sunday afternoon, for example, or at other specific prayer times that pertain to feast days and the season in the liturgical year. Through participation at holy Mass, the use of the sacraments, and throughout our daily lives, we guide our children in prayer as Pope John Paul II has said, in "intimate communion with the whole Church, through the daily realities of married and family life." We have been called as a family to live in community in our domestic churches and bring the authenticity of "our intimate communion" with the Church out into the world through our dealings with people in our society – in the parish, the workplace, and the community.

We are comforted and affirmed in our roles as prayer educators and guides to our children when we read Pope John Paul II's words in *Familiaris Consortio*, "The concrete example and living witness of parents is fundamental and irreplaceable in educating their children to pray. Only by praying together with their children can a father and mother – exercising their royal priesthood – penetrate the innermost depths of their children's hearts and leave an impression that the future events in their lives will not be able to efface."

These are very powerful words that should give us great hope and awe-inspiring encouragement for us to remain steadfast in our positions as first and foremost educators to our children. Our children will certainly hear plenty of interference outside the doors of our homes that will unfortunately contradict our teachings of the Catholic faith. Therefore, we must not become complacent and expect others to teach our children. It is our duty, period. Even if the children are enrolled in religious education classes through our parishes, we must look over the material and be sure that it is in line with the magisterium of the Church. All of this requires time and energy on a parent's part, but it is essential. We will ultimately answer to Our Lord about our teachings and any other teachings to our children. We will receive all the grace necessary to fulfill this holy and weighty obligation. It is also a great privilege to be given this task of helping form the consciences and souls of human beings, guiding them on the narrow path that leads to heaven!

"Only by praying together with their children can a father and mother – exercising their royal priesthood – penetrate the innermost depths of their children's hearts and leave an impression that the future events in their lives will not be able to efface."

1. How is the Christian family "vivified by the Lord Jesus?"

_____

_____

_____

_____

_____

2. According to Pope John Paul II in Familiaris Consortio, how does Our Lord call the family into a dialogue with him?

_____

_____

_____

_____

3. How can a Christian family be sanctified and sanctify the ecclesial community and the world?

_____

_____

_____

_____

_____

4. Why do you think the Christian family is called a "priestly people?"

_____

_____

_____

_____

_____

5. In what areas do you facilitate family prayer throughout the day?

_____

_____

_____

_____

_____

6. What are some areas where you can come together in a family community of prayer?

_____

_____

_____

_____

_____

Summing Up

Whether we live in a castle or a cave, our home can become a "domestic church" where our sanctification process begins. As mothers in the heart of these domestic churches, Our Lord gives us a sublime and awesome responsibility in raising our children in prayer, fostering holiness within our families. We can, and should, call upon the graces in the sacrament of marriage to receive the strength and grace we need to do our jobs well. We should strive to educate ourselves in the faith, researching our Church's teachings (as we are doing through this mother's study), so that we will be better informed and able to pass on the faith correctly to our children, never giving them a watered down or distorted version.

Thoughts to Ponder

We learn that prayer should be the foremost in our Christian minds and hearts. Prayer has to become our way of life. A life of prayer can be accomplished within every walk of life. Our Lord instructs us to pray without ceasing. Through our love for the Lord we draw close to him and desire to pray and stay in dialogue with him.

In 1 Thessalonians we are instructed to "pray constantly." St. Paul tells us to "pray at all times in the Spirit." In the Catechism we read, "We have not been commanded to work, to keep watch and to fast constantly, but it has been laid down that we are to pray without ceasing" (CCC, 2742).

The Catechism tells us that to overcome the battle with laziness and dullness during prayer we need to be "humble, trusting, and persevering" in our love. "This love opens our hearts to three enlightening and life-giving facts of faith about prayer." I have added a fourth by Blessed Teresa of Calcutta.

I. "It is always possible to pray." St John Chrysostom tells us, "It is possible to offer fervent prayer even while walking in public or strolling alone, or seated in your shop…while buying or selling… or even while cooking" (*Ecloga de oratione* 2, 585). As mothers, we offer our lives in service to our families as a prayer.

II. "Prayer is a vital necessity." St. Alphonsus Liguori tells us, "Those who pray are certainly saved; those who do not pray are certainly damned." That is absolutely to the point! St. John Chrysostum tells us, "Nothing is equal to prayer; for what is impossible it makes possible, what is difficult, easy…. For it is impossible, utterly impossible, for the man who prays eagerly and invokes God ceaselessly ever to sin" (*De Anna* 4, 5, 666). Mothers can indeed pray, eagerly invoking God ceaselessly in all of their motherly needs.

III. **"Prayer and Christian life are inseparable."** The Catechism tells us, "Prayer and Christian life are inseparable, for they concern the same love and the same renunciation, proceeding from love; the same filial and loving conformity with the Father's plan of love; the same transforming union in the Holy Spirit who conforms us more and more to Christ Jesus; the same love for all men, the love with which Jesus has loved us. 'Whatever you ask the Father in my name, he [will] give it to you. This I command you, love one another'" (Jn 15:16-17). Mothers exist from and for God's love. Their actions and prayers that come from their loving heart will unite their lives to Christ's.

IV. **Raising our hearts to Jesus with fervor.** Blessed Teresa of Calcutta has told us, "Perfect prayer does not consist of many words but in the fervor of the desire which raises the heart to Jesus."

"He 'prays without ceasing' who unites prayer to works and good works to prayer. Only in this way can we consider as realizable the principle of praying without ceasing" (Origen, *De orat.* 12: pg 11, 452C).

Prayer

Dear Lord,

Please open my heart fully to your will in my life. Help me to recognize that my life should be an unceasing prayer to you in order that my family may become sanctified and that I may fulfill your holy will. Deepen my prayer life, my fervor of desire, and my love for you; reminding me to call upon the graces within the sacrament of my marriage so that I may guide my family with pure and holy love. Thank you for your blessings and the opportunities to serve you, dear Lord.

Amen.

7. The Basement:
The Foot of the Cross

"And for this reason

I suffer as I do. But I am not

ashamed, for I know the

one for in whom I have put

my trust, and I am

sure that he is able to guard

until that day what I have

entrusted to him."

~ 1 Timothy 1:12

PART ONE 🍃 "A LIVING LOVE HURTS"

Blessed Teresa of Calcutta has told us, "A living love hurts. Jesus, to prove his love for us, died on the Cross. The mother, to give birth to her child, has to suffer. If you really love one another properly, there must be sacrifice."

We know that a mother's love never stops. Her suffering does not end at childbirth. Therefore, just as her love never stops, her suffering couldn't possibly cease either. Why? Because it is intertwined with her self-giving love. Mothers would have to be unfeeling creatures to avoid suffering. A mother suffers every time her child experiences a diaper rash or cuts a new tooth, when her child falls down and gets hurt, whenever her child is shunned or hurt by another, or when her child is ill. And obviously she also suffered to bring her child into the world.

Suffering also visits her from lack of sleep in caring for her children throughout the night and from fatigue in caring for their every need during her days. Another form of suffering that she may endure is in sacrificing her own desires or pursuits.

The list of sacrifices and suffering is endless, as is a mother's love. If we really love our children properly, there must be sacrifice;

otherwise, there is no real love. A mother's connectedness to her child, which continues even after the umbilical cord has been severed, allows her to truly experience a sacrificial love – a love that puts her own interests and needs on hold, a love that continues to give even when it hurts. This sacrificial love begins at the moment of conception and continues throughout a mother's pregnancy, sometimes requiring the expectant mother to even risk her own health for the life of her unborn child. It may become mandatory for the mother to have complete bed rest or undergo monitoring during her pregnancy to preserve the life of her baby, which can be tiresome and sacrificial for her.

At other times, a mother sacrifices by not giving in to the desires of her child, even when it would be much easier to do so. Nevertheless, because she knows what is best for him, she admonishes him and teaches him what is right and good. When it comes to disciplining our children, I like what St. Elizabeth Ann Seton said: "When you are excited to impatience, think for a moment how much more reason God has to be angry with you than you can have for anger against any human being; and yet how constant is his patience and forbearance." Parents, of course, should always discipline their children in a loving manner, never in impatience or anger.

Our Lord is aware of her pain, hears her prayers of pleading, and will give her all of the strength and grace needed.

There may be times as children become adolescents and teens when a mother's teachings are rejected by them. This is indeed a deep pain to a mother who has showered the faith upon her children from birth. She can face this dilemma with a courageous heart and a steadfast faith, continuing her ministry and Christian example within her family with love. Our Lord is aware of her pain, hears her prayers of pleading, and will give her all of the strength and grace needed. A mother also experiences the pain of her older children leaving the "nest" for college or embarking out in the workforce on their own. A mother, with bittersweet emotion, ushers them forth, knowing that her children were only on loan to her to raise in virtue and grace, helping to form their consciences. She also realizes that her influence will remain with them throughout their lives. Our Lord has truly given mothers huge and generous hearts with which to love.

Pope John Paul II beautifully expressed a woman's strength and suffering when he said, "As we contemplate this Mother, whose heart 'a sword has pierced' (cf. Lk 2:35), our thoughts go to *all the suffering women of the world*, suffering either physically or morally. In this suffering a woman's sensitivity plays a role, even though she often succeeds in resisting suffering better than a man. It is difficult to enumerate these sufferings; it is difficult to call them all by name. We may recall her maternal care for her children, especially when they fall sick or fall into bad ways; the death of those most dear to her; the loneliness of mothers forgotten by their grown-up children; the loneliness of widows; the sufferings of women who struggle alone to make a living; and women who have been wronged and exploited. Then there are the sufferings of consciences as a result of sin, which has wounded the woman's human or maternal dignity; the wounds of consciences which do not heal easily. With these sufferings too we must place ourselves at the foot of the Cross" (*Mulieris Dignitatem*).

We live in a world that beckons us to a life of pleasure and relaxation. Advertising teases our senses and attempts to lure us into a fantasy life. We can dream of this, especially when we are exhausted and in dire need of a break. It is certainly not wrong to desire some comfort. St. Thomas Aquinas has said, "Relaxation of the mind from work consists in playful words or deeds. Therefore, it becomes a wise and virtuous person to have recourse to such things.

It is necessary at times to make use of them, in order to give rest, as it were, to the soul" (*Summa Theologica*).

However, our hearts really should want to embrace *everything* that is required of our mothering – sacrifices and all. Our true rest will come at some point, although perhaps not until our eternal reward! In the meantime, we put one foot in front of the other, seeking to serve Our Lord in our families while we pray for the graces we need, as well as an increase of faith, hope, and love. Throughout it all, thank God, we also experience deep joy!

In *Gaudium et spes* we read, "Man is divided in himself. As a result, the whole life of men, both individual and social, shows itself to be a struggle, and a dramatic one, between good and evil, between light and darkness" (13, 2). We see the need to be on guard and careful so we will not be deceived by the world's allurements to become complacent in our mothering. Throughout this *struggle* in life, we can continue to courageously walk in faith, striving for holiness.

Heroic Virtues in Our Mothering

Our dedication to our vocation of motherhood, even being dedicated to the sacrifices, can become a kind of a struggle, too. There are those individuals who don't quite understand this kind of dedication and commitment; they may try to undermine our practice of the virtues, criticizing us, perhaps jealous of our devotion. In this case, we can pray that we will be a good example, practice the virtues, and continue with our dedication. We will then respond to those individuals in a loving manner as well.

I know a mother who struggled to breast-feed her sixth baby. Her baby was not gaining weight quickly enough, which caused the breast-feeding experience that time around to be a great difficulty. This was strange to her, since the other five babies did not have this trouble. She knew that she wanted to continue to nurse her baby and provide what she felt was the best nourishment that she could give. This meant following her doctor's orders to weigh each diaper, pump her breasts to increase the milk flow, consult lactation experts, and supplement the feedings with formula to keep her baby within the correct weight range. I feel that this mother was practicing the heroic virtues by continuing in her dedication to provide her baby with breast milk while going through all that it entailed in the frustrating process. It would have been far easier for her to give up. Even so, there were some who said that this mother was only thinking of herself because she continued to nurse her baby. We cannot please everyone, and we should realize this so that we can unflinchingly continue to love heroically within our families. Never mind what others think.

On a more dramatic level, perhaps, is the example of St. Gianna Molla, who gave her life for her unborn baby. During her pregnancy, Gianna required surgery for a tumor to save her own life. Not wanting to chance hurting her unborn baby, she opted against the surgery. Her baby was born perfectly healthy, but sadly, Gianna died one week later. Each of these scenarios of mothers giving of themselves, whether in a small, sacrificial manner or a more dramatic one, are examples of mothers truly practicing the heroic virtues required of mothers by Our Lord at various times throughout their lives.

There may be times during a mother's vocation when she experiences the deep sorrow of losing one of her babies through miscarriage. Only a mother in this situation can truly understand this painful loss. Her baby, who was once living within her womb – a part of her – is suddenly taken before she had the pleasure of holding him or her in her arms. Her expectations of having that child in her life have been snatched from her without warning. Our Lord knows his reasons. We are left only with the hope that babies taken from us in miscarriage go straight into the arms of Jesus and

Mary. Another anguish that a mother may suffer is losing a child at birth or when a child of any age dies – a deep sorrow felt straight through the heart, which may seem almost impossible to heal.

Heroic virtue is defined by John A. Hardon, SJ, in his *Pocket Catholic Dictionary* as "the performance of extraordinary virtuous actions with readiness and over a period of time. The moral virtues are exercised with ease, while faith, hope, and charity are practiced to an eminent degree. The presence of such virtues is required by the Church as the first step toward canonization. The person who has practiced heroic virtue is declared to be Venerable, and is called 'Servant of God.'" This is a subject well worth pondering. There are many instances in a mother's life in which she can strive to practice heroic virtues, which will please Our Lord very much.

When we consider our Blessed Mother Mary and how she mothered her own Son, we see that she followed him to the foot of the Cross. Let's take a few moments to read John 19: 25-28. The Blessed Mother happily partook in all of the joys of mothering Jesus, yet she did not attempt to escape the deep sorrows. Equally, she embraced them also for love of her Son. We mothers can pray that we will be able to emulate our Blessed Mother's great virtues in our own vocations as mothers.

1. *Why should sacrifice be united with the beauty of love?*

_____

_____

_____

_____

_____

_____

_____

_____

2. *What are some areas in my mothering where my love becomes sacrificial?*

_____

_____

_____

_____

_____

_____

_____

_____

3. Is it natural to want to suffer?

_____

_____

_____

_____

_____

_____

_____

_____

4. What are three ways in which I can practice heroic virtues in my mothering?

_____

_____

_____

_____

_____

_____

_____

_____

PART TWO A MOTHER'S BEATITUDES: PARADOXICAL
PROMISES THAT SUSTAIN OUR HOPE

The French word "beatitude," from the Latin stem *beautitud*
(from *beatus*), is defined as "blessed." Another definition for
"beatitude" is "bliss, or extreme happiness and serenity." Let's
keep this in mind as we discuss a mother's beatitudes and later
discover why they may take on this meaning of "blessed," "bliss,"
or "extreme happiness."

First of all, why would we discuss "bliss" and "serenity" while we are
discussing a seemingly contradictory chapter on "selfless love" and "the
foot of the Cross"? The Catechism tells us, "The Beatitudes are at the
heart of Jesus' preaching. They take up the promises made to the chosen
people since Abraham. The Beatitudes fulfill the promises by ordering
them no longer merely to the possession of a territory, but to the kingdom
of heaven" (CCC, 1716). Father Hardon described the Beatitudes in
his *Pocket Catholic Dictionary* as "the promises of happiness made by
Christ to those who faithfully accept his teaching and follow his divine
example." He also taught that the Beatitudes "are expressions of the
New Covenant, where happiness is assured already in this life, provided
a person totally gives himself to the imitation of Christ."

Take a few moments to read Matthew 5:3-12. You have probably read the Beatitudes many times and are familiar with the words. However, before continuing here, read them through until the end again anyway. Allow the Holy Spirit to inspire and enlighten you as you read in a prayerful frame of mind. Take your time.

"The Beatitudes depict the countenance of Jesus Christ and portray his charity. They express the vocation of the faithful associated with the glory of his Passion and Resurrection; they shed light on the actions and attitudes characteristic of the Christian life; they are the paradoxical promises that sustain our hope in the midst of tribulations; they proclaim the blessings and rewards already secured, however dimly, for Christ's disciples; they have begun in the lives of the Virgin Mary and all the saints" (CCC, 1717). Amazing words to ponder! Again, we are reminded that our Church teaches us so well through our Catechism.

So we see that within the Beatitudes lies the paradox. We are reassured that our hope will be sustained by God's promises in the midst of everything, no matter how difficult and trying – the blessings and rewards have *already* been secured. What amazing words and promises to take to our mother's hearts!

Our Lord provides us grace to understand the Beatitudes if we take our time, pray, and truly want to understand. The Beatitudes "reveal the goal of human existence, the ultimate end of human acts; God calls us to his own beatitude" (CCC, 1719). The Beatitudes make us partakers of the divine nature and of eternal life. We read in 2 Peter 1:3-4, "His divine power has given us everything needed for life and godliness, through the knowledge of him who called us by his own glory and goodness. Thus he has given us, through these things, his precious and very great promises, so that through them you may escape from the corruption that is in the world because of lust, and may become participants of the divine nature." Once we can grasp the meaning of the Beatitudes, we can strive to apply that knowledge to our lives.

We can be comforted with the knowledge that Our Lord's promises to us will never be broken. When we live our lives by the Beatitudes, Our Lord gives us the keys to become partakers in the divine nature and eternal life. He gives us the means to escape from the corruption of the world. Let's read through the Beatitudes again:

"Blessed are the poor in spirit, for theirs is the kingdom of heaven.

Blessed are those who mourn, for they shall be comforted.

Blessed are the meek, for they shall inherit the earth.

Blessed are those who hunger and thirst for righteousness, for they shall be satisfied.

Blessed are the merciful, for they shall obtain mercy.

Blessed are the pure in heart, for they shall see God.

Blessed are the peacemakers, for they shall be called sons of God.

Blessed are those who are persecuted for righteousness' sake, for theirs is the kingdom of heaven.

Blessed are you when men revile you and persecute you and utter all kinds of evil against you falsely on my account.

Rejoice and be glad, for your reward is great in heaven."

The Beatitudes confront us with "decisive moral choices." We are invited to "purify our hearts of bad instincts and to seek the love of God above all else. [The Beatitudes teach] us that true happiness is not found in riches or well-being, in human power, or in any human achievement – however beneficial it may be – such as science, technology, and art, or indeed in any creature, but in God alone, the source of every good and of all love" (CCC, 1723).

Through the course of our everyday lives, as we mother our children we can pause to consider our many blessings woven into the intricate tapestry of motherhood – tribulations, challenges, and all. We can seek to "purify our hearts" and rejoice and be glad, knowing that our dear Lord will indeed come through with his promises to us!

1. What do the Beatitudes promise me personally? (You may want to read them over again while thinking about your daily life.)

_____

_____

_____

_____

_____

_____

_____

2. How is my hope sustained as a mother living her life through the Beatitudes?

_____

_____

_____

_____

_____

_____

_____

_____

3. In what ways might the life of a Christian mother differ from the life of a secular person?

_____

_____

_____

_____

_____

_____

_____

4. How can I go to "the foot of the Cross" with my family?

_____

_____

_____

_____

_____

_____

_____

Summing Up

Although motherhood is undoubtedly a vocation bursting with joy, we must also acknowledge that because of the very nature of the service to others involved with connected hearts, it is certainly also a vocation heaving with sacrifice and suffering. These sacrifices are essential, and actually beautiful, in the rearing of the family. Mothers can unite their prayers to the sufferings of Jesus on the Cross, and they can pray for the graces necessary to mother with pure love, even when it's sacrificial and painful. As mothers, we can and should also call upon our Blessed Mother Mary for her magnificent intercessory prayer that will no doubt sustain us throughout all of our difficulties.

In the words of Blessed Teresa of Calcutta, "Mary, Mother of Jesus, be a Mother to me now."

Thoughts to Ponder

We are prodded to strive for holiness throughout our days, "step-by-step." The Catechism tells us, "The Decalogue, the Sermon on the Mount, and the apostolic catechesis describe for us the paths that lead to the kingdom of heaven. Sustained by the grace of the Holy Spirit, we tread them step-by-step, by everyday acts. By the working of the Word of Christ, we slowly bear fruit in the Church to the glory of God" (CCC,1724; cf. Mt 13:3-23). As we work through our everyday joys and sufferings, "step-by-step" we are sustained by God's grace, the inspiration of the Holy Spirit, and the intercession of the Blessed Mother and the saints during our loving acts of service to our families.

"Do all things without murmuring and arguing, so that you may be blameless and innocent, children of God without blemish in the midst of a crooked and perverse generation, in which you shine like stars in the world" (Phil 2:14-15) – here is another call to live a virtuous life, so contrary to what the world beckons us to do.

Let us also reflect on Pope John Paul II's words in *Mulieris Dignitatem:* On the Dignity and Vocation of Women:

"*When a woman is in travail she has sorrow,* because her hour has come; but when she is delivered of the child, *she no longer remembers the anguish,* for joy that a child is born into the world' (Jn 16:21). The first part of Christ's words refer to the 'pangs of childbirth' which belong to the heritage of original sin; at the same time these words indicate the *link that exists between the woman's motherhood and the Paschal Mystery.* For this mystery also indicates the Mother's sorrow at the foot of the Cross – the Mother who through faith shares in the amazing mystery of her Son's 'self-emptying': This is perhaps the deepest 'kenosis' of faith in human history...but the words of the Gospel about the woman who suffers when the time comes for her to give birth to her child, immediately afterwards express *joy*: it is *'the joy that a child is born into the world.'* This joy too is referred to the Paschal Mystery, to the joy which is communicated to the Apostles *on the day of Christ's Resurrection:* 'So you have sorrow now' (these words were said the day before the Passion); 'but I will see you again and your hearts will rejoice, and no one will take your joy from you'" (*Mulieris Dignitatem*, 19; Jn 16:22-23).

Oh dear Lord,

Thank you for all of your blessings and love. Help me to
realize that to love properly sacrifice must always exist.
Help me to live the life of the Beatitudes that a mother is
sublimely called to. You have taught us about the struggle in
life between good and evil; give me strength, Lord, to always
choose the good for the betterment of my own soul, as
well as to benefit my family and the world.

PRAYER
thank you for all of your blessings...

You generously
promised us that
our hearts will
rejoice and our joy
will remain with
us, never to be taken
from us. Give us the
ability to escape from
the corruption of
the world, and fill
us with unparalleled
hope in a seemingly
hopeless world.
Thank you, dear
Lord, for your love!
Amen.

8. The Porch:
An Overflowing Chalice of Love

"Once again the

Gospel says to us that

the love, from the heart of

God and operating

through the heart of the man,

is the force that renews

the world."

~ Pope Benedict XVI

November 4, 2007

PART ONE  BE KIND AND MERCIFUL

"Be kind and merciful. Let no one ever come to you
without leaving better and happier."

– Blessed Teresa of Calcutta

A mother loves with all of her heart. Her entire vocation is one of utter love. However, a mother's love does not stop flowing at the doors of her home. When she is out in the world, she couldn't possibly hide the love that "shows" upon her sleeves, which compels her to mother others with that same love that epitomizes her soul. The chalice of her motherly heart overflows with love into the world by way of the neighborhood, the circle of the ecclesial community, and in society. This love from the heart of God that is manifested through the mother "is the force that renews the world," according to Pope Benedict XVI. I find those words from Pope Benedict very amazing and extremely encouraging.

It is interesting and liberating to know that Our Lord Jesus transcended the norms of his own culture when he walked this earth, treating women with great tenderness and compassion. Pope John Paul II pointed out Jesus' great love for women when he said in *Mulieris Dignitatem*, "It is universally admitted – even by people with a critical attitude towards the Christian message – that *in the eyes of his contemporaries Christ became a promoter of women's true dignity* and of the *vocation* corresponding to this dignity. At times this caused wonder, surprise, often to the point of scandal: 'They marveled that he was talking with a woman' (Jn 4:27), because this behavior differed from that of his contemporaries. Even Christ's own disciples 'marveled.'" Jesus' great love for women is very apparent when reading and studying the Scriptures.

Additionally, in that same letter, Pope John Paul II recounts many of the women whom Jesus touched, healed, and praised, saying, "Your faith has made you well" (Mk 5:34), and "O woman, great is your faith! Be it done for you as you desire" to the Canaanite mother wanting a healing for her daughter (Mt 15:28). Women often were mentioned in the parables that Jesus told to the people of his day. Jesus consistently shows love to the holy and sinner alike. Jesus speaks to women, and they understand him. "There is a true resonance of mind and heart, a response of faith. Jesus expresses appreciation and admiration for this distinctly 'feminine' response, as in the case of the Canaanite woman (cf. Mt 15:28)" (*Mulieris Dignitatem* V, 15).

Many of the women who encountered Jesus also accompanied him as he journeyed with the Apostles and they, along with the Apostles, proclaimed the Good News of the Kingdom of God. We know that "from the beginning of Christ's mission, women show to him and to his mystery a special *sensitivity which is characteristic* of their *femininity*" (*Mulieris Dignitatem* V, 16). Women were the first at Jesus' tomb to find it empty. They were first to hear, "He is not here. He has risen, as he said" (Mt 28:6). They were the first to embrace Jesus' feet (cf. Mt 28:1-10; Lk 24:8-11). Scripture also tells us that Mary Magdalene was the first eyewitness to the Risen Christ as well as the first to bear witness to him before the Apostles. Pope John Paul II noted that this is another instance of "Christ entrusting divine truths to women as well as men."

"Everything that has been said so far about Christ's attitude to women confirms and clarifies, in the Holy Spirit, the truth about the 'equality,' since both of them – the woman as much as the man – are created in the image and likeness of God. Both of them are equally capable of receiving the outpouring of divine truth and love in the Holy Spirit. Both receive his salvific and sanctifying 'visits'" (*Mulieris Dignitatem* V, 16).

Women possess many gifts from God, and among them are: a loving heart, deep tenderness, patience, sensitivity, great insight and intuition, and the ability to undergo suffering for the sake of another. Because of these many inviting and generous gifts, it is natural for people to be drawn to women for their advice, consolation, and their warm shoulder of tenderness. Therefore, a mother may also "mother" others beside her own children. In actuality, her motherly heart embraces all human life. I know some married Catholic women who were not able to physically have children and did not have the opportunity to adopt. However, I see very clearly that they are busy mothering others around them in the workplace or neighborhood with their loving woman's heart.

"A woman's dignity is closely connected with the love which she receives by the very reason of her femininity; it is likewise connected with the love which she gives in return. The truth about the person and about love is thus confirmed with regard to the truth about the person, we must turn again to the

Second Vatican Council: 'Man, who is the only creature on earth that God willed for its own sake, cannot fully find himself except through a sincere gift of self.' This applies to every human being, as a person created in God's image, whether man or woman. This ontological affirmation also indicated the ethical dimension of a person's vocation. Woman can only find herself by giving love to others" (*Mulieris Dignitatem*).

Yet again, we are reminded that we mothers *find* ourselves within our service to others – our loving of others through our "sincere gift of self." The fruits of a mother's vocation are not only manifested within her home, but also within society, blossoming forth from the sincere gift of herself.

Guarding and Transmitting Virtues and Values

The Catholic Church tells us that a Christian family is "the first and vital cell of society" (*Familiaris Consortio*). The Synod Fathers recalled that the family is "the place and origin and most effective means for humanizing and personalizing society: It makes an original contribution in depth to building up the world, by making possible a life that is properly speaking human, in particular by guarding and transmitting virtues and 'values.'"

The Second Vatican Council states that, in the family, "the various generations come together and help one another to grow wiser and to harmonize personal rights with other requirements of social living" (*Gravissimum educationis*, 3). It's too bad that in our culture today, many families have been broken up through divorce, work transfers, and other situations, which has caused the family to become disconnected from its extended family. When I grew up, I was surrounded by an extended family of aunts, uncles, cousins, and my grandmother (my other grandparents were deceased), all who helped to shape my life. Families need to do their best to stay connected with family. I know of one family where the father refused a work transfer that promised greater pay and perks in order to keep his family connected with their extended family. They had to struggle a bit for a short while due to a decrease in his paycheck; however, they made it work and are happier for it.

In *Familiaris Consortio*, Pope John Paul II discussed how our society is "running the risk of becoming more and more depersonalized and standardized and therefore inhuman and dehumanizing, with the negative results of many forms of escapism – such as alcoholism, drugs and even terrorism – the family possesses and continues still to release formidable energies capable of taking man out of his anonymity, keeping him conscious of his personal dignity, enriching him with deep humanity and actively placing him, in his uniqueness and unrepeatability, within the fabric of society" (FC, III, 43).

What does all of this really mean? First of all, a Christian family is a gift from God. It is a group of individuals that God himself has chosen to be connected together in the blessedness of a family. Each child that is conceived is "born" into that family, whether or not that soul ever sees the light of day through the birth process. Some babies are taken in miscarriage; some may be snuffed out through contraception when the method used acts as an abortifacient; and some are sadly and horribly robbed of their life in this world through the murderous act of abortion. Every conceived pregnancy is a human person and is part of a family. A real family, as stated by the Second Vatican Council, is the "various generations" coming together to "help one another to grow wiser and to harmonize personal rights with other requirements of social living." That's our job as family members – to build each other up, working together to get to heaven! Unfortunately, there are many families who do not experience the benefits of extended family nearby or within their homes. Sadly, the coming together of the many generations of families that Pope John Paul II spoke of is becoming more and more scarce.

A Christian family is a vital cell of society. When a family is dysfunctional, it affects the whole society. It's not possible to overlook the problems prevalent in our world today; they are all rooted in the lack of love in the basic unit of society – the family – which has been sadly falling apart.

Christian families are called by God to go out of their households and love their fellow human beings within the fabric of society, offering peace and perhaps a healing balm in our depersonalized and troubled world. We know that we are called by God to be a light to others in this world, leading the way to heaven. We learn from *Familiaris Consortio*, "Thus the Christian family is inspired and guided by the new law of the Spirit and, in intimate communion with the church, the kingly people; it is called to exercise its 'service' of love towards God and towards its fellow human beings. Just as Christ exercises his royal power by serving us, so also the Christian finds the authentic meaning of his participation in the kingship of his Lord in sharing his spirit and practice of service to man" *(FC, 63)*.

A mother is lovingly bound first to her duties to her family, because love naturally begins at home. We know that mothers shouldn't rush off to "share his spirit and practice of service" and care for others while neglecting the people in their own family – the ones that God has put right in their midst to care for. However, when all needs are taken care of, and if it is appropriate, mothers may carry their loving hearts out into society, helping in one capacity or another to ease the suffering in our world.

This can be accomplished through helping at a local soup kitchen, participating in a mother's group, helping a struggling family or a single mother, within a religious education setting (whether teaching or learning), assisting the elderly or unfortunate, helping with a pro-life endeavor, or volunteering in a parish ministry. Mothers must also find ways to encourage other mothers who may be struggling along in their motherhood or confused by the onslaught of mixed messages that our society directs at them regarding their worth in this world. Sadly, too often a mother's worth seems to be measured in our society by the size of her paycheck, not for her invaluable dedication and devotion to her family. We have to combat this mentality and strive to bring back the dignity that motherhood deserves by helping to change attitudes in our dealings with people. We can aid other mothers and our society with our example, our courage to speak up, and our willingness to lend a hand, thus lifting the spirits of mothers everywhere. Sometimes changing attitudes and raising the view of women's dignity is accomplished woman-to-woman, heart-to-heart. It then continues, by God's grace, throughout society. I sincerely hope that all those who participate in this study will consider how they may help in this regard.

Carrying our hearts out into the world to help others is actually answering a call from the beautiful Gospel of Matthew 25:31-46. Although there's no doubt that you are familiar with these powerful words, please take a moment to read that passage now. Afterwards, perhaps close your eyes and take a few moments to prayerfully reflect upon the passage.

In his book, *Rise, Let Us Be on Our Way*, Pope John Paul II tells us, "The laity can accomplish their vocation in the world and attain holiness not only through their active involvement in helping the poor and needy, but also by imbuing society with a Christian spirit as they carry out their professional duties and offer an example of Christian family life." The late pontiff's encouraging words give us consolation in our vocation. He helps us mothers realize that the example of our Christian family life will aid others in the world who may be searching for a deeper meaning or a way to get closer to God. Some of these individuals may not even realize that they are searching for God, yet they are drawn to the blessedness of our Christianity – of Jesus living within us. Moreover, we should be excited because, according to Pope John Paul II, as we prayerfully and faithfully live out our lives within our vocation in our households and in the world, we will attain holiness!

1. How can a mother's loving heart be a "force which renews the world"?

_____

_____

_____

_____

_____

_____

_____

_____

_____

_____

_____

_____

2. *How do women find themselves?*

3. How is a Christian family a light to the world?

_____

_____

_____

_____

_____

_____

_____

4. How can my Christian family aid society?

_____

_____

_____

_____

_____

_____

_____

_____

PART TWO ❧ LOVE KNOWS HOW TO DISCOVER THE
FACE OF CHRIST: FINDING GOD IN EACH BROTHER AND SISTER

"We should not serve the poor like they were Jesus.
We should serve the poor because they are Jesus."

– Blessed Teresa of Calcutta

Blessed Teresa of Calcutta always referred to the poor she served as "Jesus in the distressing disguise of the poorest of the poor." She was firmly convinced that Jesus lives within each and every person and that we are all called to serve Jesus in each other, especially in the poor and unfortunate.

Once when Blessed Teresa of Calcutta was asked how she could be so courageous to go out and minister to the poorest of the poor, she responded, "I would not have any [courage] if I were not convinced that each time I touch the body of a leper, a body that reeks with a foul stench, I touch Christ's body, the same Christ I receive in the Eucharist."

Without a doubt, Blessed Teresa's work with the poor was much more radical and far-reaching than the care for others that we actively engage in as mothers; however, we too are called to *see* and care for Jesus within every human being we encounter. We do this

The spiritual works of mercy are: admonish the sinner, instruct the ignorant, counsel the doubtful, comfort the sorrowful, bear wrongs patiently, forgive all injuries, and pray for the living and the dead.

by God's grace and through prayerful hearts. Blessed Teresa serves as an exemplary example of this loving service to Jesus. I feel very fortunate to have seen this holy woman in action. God has indeed blessed those of us who live in this era with the example of Mother Teresa to emulate and call upon for her intercession.

We just recently read the Gospel of Matthew (25:31-46), and we have been reminded that we are instructed by Jesus himself that when we are feeding, giving drink, visiting, and clothing – "Just as you did it to one of the least of these who are members of my family, you did it to me" – we are truly doing it to him. As Christians, we are called to *live* the corporal and spiritual works of mercy. The corporal works of mercy are: feed the hungry, give drink to the thirsty, clothe the naked, shelter the homeless, visit the sick, visit the imprisoned, and bury the dead. The spiritual works of mercy are: admonish the sinner, instruct the ignorant, counsel the doubtful, comfort the sorrowful, bear wrongs patiently, forgive all injuries, and pray for the living and the dead.

In *Familiaris Consortio*, we discover Our Lord within others outside our families and even further about our responsibility towards the whole of society. Pope John Paul II told us, "Inspired and sustained by the new commandments of love, the Christian family welcomes, respects and serves every human being, considering each one in his or her dignity as a person and a child of God.

"It should be so especially between husband and wife and within the family, through a daily effort to promote a truly personal community, initiated and fostered by an inner communion of love. This way of life should then be extended to the wider circle of the ecclesial community of which the Christian family is a part. Thanks to the love within the family, the Church can and ought to take on a more homelike or family dimension, developing a more human and fraternal style of relationships.

"Love, too, goes beyond our brothers and sisters of the same faith since 'everybody is my brother or sister.' In each individual, especially the poor, the weak, and those who suffer or are unjustly treated, love knows how to discover the face of Christ, and discover a fellow human being to be loved and served.

"In order that the family may serve man in a truly evangelical way, the instructions of the Second Vatican Council must be carefully put into practice: 'That the exercise of such charity may rise above any deficiencies in fact and even in appearance, certain fundamentals must be observed. Thus, attention is to be paid to the image of God in which our neighbor has been created, and also to Christ the Lord to whom is really offered whatever is given to a needy person'" (*Familiaris Consortio* III, 64).

Through perseverance in prayer, mothers can strive to see Jesus within their family members and also in those they minister to in one way or another throughout their daily lives. In this way, they live the Gospel message of Matthew of caring for Jesus within each human being.

1. How might I be called to serve Jesus based on his message in Matthew 23:31-46?

_____

_____

_____

_____

_____

_____

_____

2. How can I be sure that what I feel I want to do to help others out in the world is in conformity to God's holy will for me? List three or more ways in which to discern this:

_____

_____

_____

_____

_____

_____

_____

_____

_____

_____

_____

_____

_____

_____

_____

_____

_____

_____

_____

3. *How can I see Jesus living within my fellow human beings?*

_____

_____

_____

_____

_____

_____

_____

_____

4. *What can I teach my children about ministering to others?*

_____

_____

_____

_____

_____

_____

_____

_____

_____

Summing Up

Mothers possess many gifts that are giving and serving in nature. A mother's heart is naturally inclined to help and serve others. She prays to discern where Our Lord would like her to serve – apart from her service within her own family. When she knows that her family is taken care of properly, she can offer her loving heart to minister to others.

Thoughts to Ponder

"When we pray, the voice of the heart must be heard more than the proceedings from the mouth," St. Bonaventure has told us. Mothers know that their prayers are vocalized through their hearts as they actively serve their families and their fellow human beings. St. Catherine of Siena said, "You must pray the prayer of action, which is the fragrant flower of the soul. A good man [or woman] is a prayer." Our hearts are uplifted, knowing that we can truly make a difference in our families and out in the world through our loving and prayerful hearts!

Oh dear Lord,

Thank you for my life within my family. Thank you for all of the graces and blessings that you are constantly bestowing upon me. Help me to use all my gifts for your glory and the good of others. Open my eyes to see you in the "disguise" of all of those around me – my family, friends, coworkers, and neighbors. Help me to truly live your Gospel and do everything I do because of my love for you, knowing that with each person I serve, I am serving you, dear Lord. Thank you for your love!

Amen.

Prayer

9. The Patio:
Evangelizing with the Feminine Genius

"It is not enough to

discover Christ

– you must bring him

to others!"

~ Pope John Paul II

Part One ᴥ To the Ends of the Earth!

"Go into all the world
and proclaim the good news to the whole creation."

– Mk 15:16

As Christians, we are called to not only live our Christianity but we are also summoned to go forth to bring the message of the Gospel to others – "to the ends of the earth." Pope Benedict XVI explained that the Apostles were the first to follow in Jesus' steps to evangelize the world. Jesus referred to Simon, Andrew, James, and John at the Sea of Galilee as "fishers of men." Pope Benedict said, "The Apostles' adventure began as an encounter between people who opened to one another." Because they had a direct knowledge of their Master, they could bring the true message of Christ to others, not just an idea of him or their own interpretations. Their intimate relationship with Jesus enabled them to accurately and articulately convey him to those they met.

The Church gives us some wonderful words in *Familiaris Consortio* regarding the unique evangelization in and through the family: "The ministry of evangelization carried out by Christian parents is original and irreplaceable. It assumes the characteristics typical of family life itself, which should be interwoven with love, simplicity, practicality, and daily witness.

"The family must educate the children for life in such a way that each one may fully perform his or her role according to the vocation received from God. Indeed, the family that is open to transcendent values, that serves its brothers and sisters with joy, that fulfills its duties with generous fidelity, and is aware of its daily sharing in the mystery of the glorious Cross of Christ, becomes the primary and most excellent seedbed of vocations to a life of consecration to the Kingdom of God" (FC IV, 53).

When our daily witness in the family is holy, vocations of holiness will indeed blossom. We call upon the graces in the sacrament of marriage as well as our baptism and confirmation graces to be witnesses of Christ – spreading the faith to others. "The sacrament of marriage takes up and re-proposes the task of defending and spreading the faith, a task that has its roots in baptism and confirmation, and makes Christian married couples and parents witnesses of Christ 'to the end of the earth,' missionaries, in the true and proper sense, of love and life" (FC IV, 54). Isn't it wonderful that as we are parenting our children, we are also involved in our God-given duties of defending and spreading our faith? This can happen naturally within the walls of our domestic churches and when we are out in society as an example and witness of our faith.

Pope John Paul II told us in *Mulieris Dignitatem*, "Holy women are an incarnation of the feminine ideal." He also often referred to women's "feminine genius." He said, "The Church gives thanks *for all the manifestations of the feminine 'genius'* which have appeared in the course of history, in the midst of all peoples and nations; she gives thanks for all the charisms which the Holy Spirit distributes to women in the history of the People of God, for all the victories which she owes to their faith, hope and charity: she gives thanks for all *the fruits of the feminine* holiness" (MD, 27).

We must use our feminine genius within our families and in the world. We mothers must deepen our relationship with Jesus every chance we have if we want to be able to truly bring Jesus to others – and follow in the footsteps of the Apostles. We will accomplish this through prayer and a deep desire to come to know Our Lord more intimately. As mothers, our evangelization to the ends of the earth begins within our hearts, deepening our love for the Lord and growing ever closer to him. He will increase our faith, hope, and love. We need to ask him on a daily basis. We then can bring Jesus to others – first within our own homes through our love, word, and example, while being patient with our state of life. Because of our active role with our little ones who need our constant care, our evangelization "to the ends of the earth" will mostly be to the ends of our household during certain seasons of our mothering. However, this is absolutely essential, and Our Lord is certainly working there in a way that is much greater than we can ever imagine.

Pope John Paul II told us in *Familiaris Consortio*, "Christian families offer a special contribution to the missionary cause of the church by fostering missionary vocations among their sons and daughters and, more generally, 'by training their children from childhood to recognize God's love for all people'" (*FC* IV, 54 and Second Vatican Ecumenical Council, Dogmatic Constitution on the Church, Decree on the Apostolate for the Laity, *Apostolicam Actuositatem*, 30.) We are reminded that one or more of our children may have a calling to religious life, and we should pray for them in this regard, as well as to encourage it.

Parents are living witnesses of their Christian faith within their home and society. Another form of missionary activity that is utilized within the home happens "when some member of the family does not have the faith or does not practice it with consistency. In such a case, the other members must give him or her a living witness of their own faith in order to encourage and support him or her along the path towards full acceptance of Christ the Savior.

"Animated in its own inner life by missionary zeal, the Church of the home is also called to be a luminous sign of the presence of Christ and of his love for those who are 'far away,' for families who do not yet believe, and for those Christian families who no longer live in accordance with the faith that they once received. The Christian family is called to enlighten 'by its example and its witness…those who seek the truth'" (*Familiaris Consortio* IV, 54 and Second Vatican Ecumenical Council, Dogmatic Constitution on the Church, *Lumen Gentium*, 35; cf. Decree on the Apostolate of the Laity, *Apostolicam Actuositatem*, 11).

One instance of our missionary example in the home is at the family dinner table when we say grace before meals and follow that with a family prayer in common at the table. Members of the family and visitors to the household who may not be practicing Catholics may be edified by the family prayers, even if they do not indicate it. We never know what kind of impact prayer will have on another. Our prayers, voiced in the presence of non-praying individuals, could actually be the spark that helps to reignite the fire of love for Jesus in their hearts. It may also introduce Our Lord to those who do not already know him. Our prayers, said naturally in the family setting of our domestic churches, are more powerful than we envision. This same love and prayer goes with us when we are out and about in the world. A very effective means of our family evangelization out in the world happens very naturally as we and our children bow our heads after blessing ourselves with the Sign of the Cross when we are out at a restaurant before eating our meal. We are not trying to draw attention to ourselves; we are merely asking the good Lord to bless our food. In so doing, someone present who may not have any other contact with prayer in their lives may see us praying, and by God's grace, begin to think twice about his or her life and where they are headed. God is in control, and we ask him each day to work through us so that others can be brought to him. We leave it all in his hands and trust that his graces and blessings are flowing.

"Joy is a net of love by which you can catch souls!"

I am again reminded of Blessed Teresa of Calcutta's message, "Joy is a net of love by which you can catch souls!" She insisted that the sisters in her order, the

Missionaries of Charity, all over the world care for others with a joyful loving heart and a smile. I was very impressed with the sisters' joyful attitude when I met each one of them at the various convents that I visited. Blessed Teresa also used to tell me, "Keep the joy of the Lord as your strength," and "Keep the joy of loving Jesus ever burning in your heart and share this joy with others by your thoughtful love and humble service." The joy of Jesus' love was vitally important to her in her ministry in caring for the poorest of the poor. She believed that joy could be a healer and a very welcome attitude to those who are accustomed to misery and pain. She also said, "I believe in person-to-person; every person is Christ for me, and since there is only one Jesus, that person is the one person in the world at that moment."

Remember that saying, "When Mama ain't happy, ain't nobody happy"? Pardon the grammar, please, but I think you get the point. While we are busy taking care of our families and ministering to others, let's not forget to smile and bring that contagious joy to all of those who surround us. A simple smile can warm hearts and change perspectives. The joy behind our smiles will attract people to the blessedness of our Christianity. There are challenging situations when mustering up a smile is difficult to do. Running a busy household can be stressful and exhausting at times; however, Our Lord sees and appreciates each bead of perspiration and knows each little or big pain that may jab at our hearts during our acts of love to our family. The knowledge that he sees and appreciates our labors of love should be enough to summon our smile and a happy response to our families. Yes, we are human; we have feelings that can undergo hurt and bodies that can get weary. Let's try to take care of ourselves and get proper rest when possible, so that we are better able to care for those whom God has entrusted to our care. Let's strive to do our work without grumbling or complaining – rather, let's do it with happy hearts, radiating our joy to others!

1. How do you think God is calling you as a mother to evangelize?

_____

_____

_____

_____

_____

_____

_____

_____

2. How do I "tap into" my feminine genius – my feminine holiness?

_____

_____

_____

_____

_____

_____

_____

_____

_____

3. List three or more ways in which you evangelize within your "domestic church."

_____

_____

_____

_____

_____

_____

4. As we are parenting our children during our daily lives, how are we also involved in our God-given duties of defending and spreading our faith? List as many instances as you can.

_____

_____

_____

_____

_____

_____

_____

_____

Part Two ⟳ Called to Be a Luminous Sign of the Presence of Christ

"Animated in its own inner life by missionary zeal,
the Church of the home is also called to be a luminous sign of the
presence of Christ and of his love."

– Familiaris Consortio

Our Lord allows us to participate in his kingship as we share his spirit and practice of service to mankind. We learn from *Familiaris Consortio*, "Thus, the Christian family is inspired and guided by the new law of the Spirit [the new commandment of love] and, in intimate communion with the Church, the kingly people, it is called to exercise its 'service' of love towards God and towards its fellow human beings. Just as Christ exercises his royal power by serving us, so also the Christian finds the authentic meaning of his participation in the kingship of the Lord in sharing his spirit and practice of service to man. Christ has communicated this power to his disciples that they may be established in royal freedom and that by self-denial and a holy life they might conquer the reign of sin in themselves (cf. Rom 6:12). Further, he has shared this power so that by serving him in their fellow human beings they might through humility and patience lead their brothers and sisters to that King whom to serve is to reign. For the Lord wishes to spread his kingdom by means of the laity also, a kingdom of truth and life, a kingdom of holiness and grace, a kingdom of justice, love and peace. In this kingdom, creation itself will be delivered out of its slavery to corruption and into the freedom of the glory of the children of God" *(FC* IV, 63; cf. Rom 8:21). These are powerful words that we can meditate upon.

Pope John Paul II told us, "Today the world is 'hungrier and thirstier' than ever for motherhood which, physically or spiritually, is woman's great vocation." In addition to bringing Jesus to our family members throughout our daily lives, we bring him to others in our dealings with people outside our homes, "mothering" them in some way while never neglecting our duties to our families in the process.

I love this verse from Deuteronomy: "Hear, O Israel: The Lord is our God, the Lord alone. You shall love the Lord your God with all your heart, and with all your soul, and with all your might. Keep these words that I am commanding you today in your heart. Recite them to your children and talk about them when you are at home and when you are away, when you lie down and when you rise. Bind them as a sign on your hand, fix them as an emblem on your forehead, and write them on the doorposts of your house and on your gates (Dt 6:4-9). I'd say that these holy words call us to be very outspoken and profess our faith and love for God often and everywhere! While we won't necessarily write our love for God across our foreheads, our motherly intuition and our feminine genius will weave its way through our words and actions to fulfill our response to this admonition. Opportunities to show our love for Our Lord and evangelize others surround us always – every day, in all our walks of life.

We can also read the "Ode to a Capable Wife" in Proverbs 31:10-31. The capable wife is described as "far more precious than jewels." She is described in detail within these twenty-one verses in Proverbs, which I hope you will read. One that stands out for this particular discussion on being a witness out in the world, called to be a luminous sign of the presence of Christ, is: "She opens her hand to the poor, and reaches out her hands to the needy" (verse 20).

Opportunities to show our love for Our Lord and evangelize others surround us always – every day, in all our walks of life.

While remembering that our example speaks much louder than our words, we can feel confident that even out at the grocery story, the post office, the bank, and other places where we do our errands, God is sure to put people in our path. A simple smile, a door held open, a listening ear to someone we meet who has an immediate need, giving a hand to a mother with many children in tow – all kinds of situations arise in which we can lend a hand – and most importantly, lend our hearts. Even in these little things, Our Lord is working. Through little acts of kindness, miracles do happen. A simple smile and a kind word may have been just the little act of love that a lonely person absolutely needed so as not to fall into despair that particular day. At other times, our evangelizing out in the world is more complex through our explanation of Christ's teachings when the opportunity arises. All of this can be accomplished without pretension or showiness – rather, with caring hearts we can reach out where there is a need and allow Our Lord to work through us. Words and gestures are powerful, especially when acting with a pure and loving heart. Conversely, someone acting from a selfish perspective can also powerfully affect another, but in a negative way.

I like to use the example of how one word I said, by God's grace, worked a miracle in someone's heart that affected her whole family and brought them into the Catholic Church. One morning, in our usual rush to get ready for school, my youngest child, Mary-Catherine, who was about three years old at the time, insisted upon wearing a fancy dress that day. I didn't fuss about her fashion choice too much because I liked that she loved to dress femininely. I thought, *How dirty could she get in just a few minutes out at the bus stop?* So, while I was at the bus stop, saying good-bye to my older children as they boarded the school bus, my neighbor complimented my daughter about her appearance.

"You look so beautiful in that dress, Mary-Catherine!" she said, while Mary-Catherine twirled around.

"It's actually her church dress, but she really wanted to wear it this morning," I explained.

That's when my neighbor started to cry. I was puzzled and stunned. I had no idea what was going on. However, as my neighbor sobbed, she began to tell me of a deep pain that she had been holding in her heart for about eight years. She explained that her father, upon his deathbed, made her promise to get her baby boy baptized. She looked him in the eye and promised him. But eight years had passed, and holy water had never caressed his head; her son had never been blessed with the sacrament of baptism. She told me that she felt that it was much too late now.

I was very happy to be able to assist my dear neighbor, first by comforting her in her tearful time by offering a hug. And then, I told her that it was never too late, and that, contrary to what she thought, the priests at our parish would welcome her and her son with open arms, with no scolding whatsoever. I offered to call our pastor to "break the ice" for her to follow up with a phone call. The ending to the story is that this boy was baptized shortly thereafter, and his mother came back into the Church! During his religious education classes, his mother volunteered at the parish office, which helped her to feel connected to the parish community and the whole Catholic Church. God is so good! That one word, "church," said at the right time, in the right place, brought about this miracle by God's grace. I'm so happy that he occasionally gives us glimpses when he is at work, as he did with me in this "one word" miracle situation. We need to trust that God is always at work; he is always asking us to open our hearts and allow him to use us as his instruments.

Go and Teach and "Become All Things to All Men"

"But you take courage!
Do not let your hands be weak, for your work shall be rewarded."
– 2 Chr 15:7

The Catechism reminds us to be sensitive to the unique needs of others, whether in our role of teaching the faith through religious education, or while we are out mingling with people and teaching the faith through our words and actions. Even though we feel the urge to win everyone to Christ, we need to realize that not all are at the same level of learning. We may need to adjust our approach.

"Whoever teaches must become 'all things to all men' (1 Cor 9:22), to win everyone to Christ.... Above all, teachers must not imagine that a single kind of soul has been entrusted to them, and that consequently it is lawful to teach and form equally all the faithful in true piety with one and the same method! Let them realize that some are in Christ as newborn babes, others as adolescents, and still others as adults in full command of their powers.... Those who are called to the ministry of preaching must suit their words to the maturity and understanding of their hearers, as they hand on the teaching of the mysteries of faith and the rules of moral conduct" (CCC, Prologue VI, Roman Catechism, Preface, 11; cf. 1 Cor 9:22;

1 Pet 2:2). Isn't Mother Church brilliant to consider the needs of everyone?

Think about the woman at the well in John 4:1-30. The Samaritan woman went to the well to retrieve water for her family. Jesus went to the well to offer the "living water." After some discussion between the woman and Jesus, which incidentally was unheard of at the time, especially since the woman was a Samaritan, the woman admitted to her life of sin. She realized then whom she was speaking with, and she accepted the living water from Jesus so that her innate thirst for the truth would be satiated. She dropped her bucket near the well and ran back to tell her people about Jesus, becoming a missionary.

In the same way, we women can leave the bucket of "stuff" behind – the clutter that fills our minds and our homes – distracting us from receiving the living water that is essential for survival. We, then, can act as missionaries, just like the woman at the well, and bring Jesus to others. We may also want to consider whether or not we may be too busy at times "fetching the water" to actually hear what Our Lord is trying to tell us. I am referring to being overbooked with activities and surrounded with so much noise that we cannot hear Our Lord. We have to find opportunities to pause and listen.

St. Augustine described his daily life in this quote, which was also used by Pope Benedict XVI in his encyclical, *Spe Salvi*. St. Augustine said, "The turbulent have to be corrected, the faint-hearted cheered up, the weak supported; the Gospel's opponents need to be refuted, its insidious enemies guarded against; the unlearned need to be taught, the indolent stirred up, the argumentative checked; the proud must be put in their place, the desperate set on their feet, those engaged in quarrels reconciled; the needy have to be helped, the oppressed to be liberated, the good to be encouraged, the bad to be tolerated; all must be loved" (*Sermo* 340, 3: *PL* 38, 1484; cf. F. Van der Meer, *Augustine the Bishop*, p. 268). In our own motherly ways, and with God's love and joy in our hearts, we strive to care for all of these people as well.

Pope John Paul II reminded us of our calling to be a strong witness to the world and with an even greater spiritual and apostolic boldness. He said, "The Church relies especially on the witness and contribution of Christian families to fulfill her urgent mission. Indeed, in the face of the dangers and difficulties that beset the family institution, she invites families to have greater spiritual and apostolic boldness, knowing that the family is called to be 'a sign of unity for the world' and thus to bear witness to 'the Kingdom

and peace of Christ, towards which the whole world is journeying'"
(Angelus, Feast of the Holy Family, December 30, 2001). Our
family's example in our own domestic church and while out in the
world can make a tremendous impact on society.

Blessed Teresa of Calcutta explains to us, "Often you see small
and big wires, new and old, cheap and expensive electric cables that
are useless, for until the current passes through them there will be
no light. The wires are you and me; the current is God. We have the
power to let the current pass through us – to use us – or refuse to be
used and allow darkness to spread." Such poignant words to ponder
regarding our responsibility to spread God's light! It's a choice we
make each and every day. Are we choosing darkness or light?

1. How can I serve Jesus in my fellow human beings so that, through humility and patience, I may lead my brothers and sisters to that King whom "to serve is to reign"?

_____

_____

_____

_____

_____

2. What are three ways in which I can bring Jesus to the people in society – in my community and my world?

_____

_____

_____

_____

_____

3. How do I become "all things to all men" and bring everyone to Christ?

_____

_____

_____

_____

_____

4. How can I imitate the woman at the well?

_____

_____

_____

_____

_____

_____

_____

_____

5. How is the church of the home a "luminous sign of the presence of Christ and of his love?"

_____

_____

_____

_____

_____

_____

_____

_____

Summing Up

Let us women take Pope John Paul II's words to heart, "Dear sisters...reflect carefully on...the 'genius of women'...to let this genius be more fully expressed in the life of society as a whole, as well as in the life of the Church" (*1995 Letter to Women*).

We know that as Christians, we have a duty to not only live the Gospel, but we also need to bring it to others – first within the heart of our own homes, where our dear Lord has placed us to work out our salvation and our family's, and afterwards, out into the world whenever we are called to be a witness there – at the grocery store, on the playground, in the workplace, or at the soup kitchen. Blessed Teresa has said, "Our works of love are nothing but works of peace. Let us do them with greater love and efficiency, each in his or her own work, in daily life, at home, with one's neighbor."

The Catechism tells us, "Christ chose to be born and grow up in the bosom of the holy family of Joseph and Mary. The Church is nothing other than 'the family of God.' From the beginning, the core of the Church was often constituted by those who had become believers 'together with all [their] household.' When they were converted, they desired that 'their whole household' should also be saved. These families who became believers were islands of Christian life in an unbelieving world.

"In our own time, in a world often alien and even hostile to faith, believing families are of primary importance as centers of living, radiant faith. For this reason the Second Vatican Council, using an ancient expression, calls the family the *Ecclesia domestica*. It is in example...of the first heralds of the faith with regard to their children. They should encourage them in the vocation which is proper to each child, fostering with special care any religious vocation'" (CCC, 1655, 1656; *Lumen Gentium*, 11).

Thoughts to Ponder

Our Lord will use us in all instances within our homes and out in the world. St. Augustine pointed out the many and varied needs of people in our midst. Pope John Paul II reminded us that, "the ministry of evangelization carried out by Christian parents is original and irreplaceable. It assumes the characteristics typical of family life itself, which should be interwoven with love, simplicity, practicality, and daily witness." We mothers should keep these components in mind: love, simplicity, practicality, and daily witness – so that we may respond to Our Lord's call to us to evangelize.

Pope John Paul II has encouraged us, "Indeed, the family that is open to transcendent values, that serves its brothers and sisters with joy, that fulfills its duties with generous fidelity, and is aware of its daily sharing in the mystery of the glorious Cross of Christ becomes the primary and most excellent seedbed of vocations to a life of consecration to the Kingdom of God."

How will we respond to everything and everyone that touches our lives? Will we be a sign of unity to the world and bear witness to the kingdom and peace of Christ? Will all of our responses be rooted in Christ's love? As Father John A. Hardon, SJ, my former spiritual director and friend, put it very succinctly, "There's work to be done!" And we can see that there's plenty of it. Our dear Lord is counting on us. Are we willing to do it?

Let us mothers also take those very special words of Pope John Paul II to heart, "Be not afraid!" as we go about our mothering. Our Lord will accompany us on our journeys if we allow him into all the rooms of our domestic churches and into our hearts!

"May Christ the Lord, the Universal King, the King of Families,
be present in every Christian home
as he was at Cana, bestowing light, joy, serenity and strength."
– Pope John Paul II, *Familiaris Consortio*

Prayer

Oh dear Lord,

Please open my heart to truly desire to serve
you with a greater love and passion. Help me to see
when it is appropriate for me to go out of my home
to evangelize, and when it is appropriate to be patient
with my duties within my domestic church, serving and
evangelizing there in the heart of the home. Thank you,
dear Lord, for your love and many blessings for me.
Help me to instill within my family an intense love for
you and a desire to come ever closer to you.
Help me to "be not afraid" in my mothering, teaching
me to lean on you more fully, surrendering my life to
you. Please shine through me so that I may selflessly be
your instrument and bring many others to you.
Thank you for this very beautiful vocation of motherhood!

Oh dear Lord, enlarge my heart and allow me
to be your love.

Amen.

Leader's Guide: Answers

This part of the Leader's Guide contains the answers to the questions for each chapter. Some of the answers will be personal.

1 – Our Blessed Mother Mary and Motherhood

Part One: "I Am the Handmaid of the Lord"

1. *This is a personal answer. Encourage the women to share some of their answers if they feel comfortable. You may come prepared to share yourself to "break the ice" and start the discussion.*

2. *This is a personal answer. Again, encourage the members to share some of their ideas. You may start off with part of your answer.*

3. *This is a personal answer. Encourage discussion.*

4. *The answers will vary.* Some suggestions for quieting the soul to hear God are:

   a. Setting a specific time for prayer, knowing that it may be interrupted because of small children. Nonetheless, this specific time should be sought with patience and dedication to keeping it.

   b. Find a comfortable and quiet setting to pray. Before the Blessed Sacrament is recommended but is not always possible.

   c. Ask for help from Jesus and Mary to find this quiet time and to be faithful to finding it.

   d. After your prayers of petition and thanksgiving are said, be sure that you don't rush off from prayer if you can spare the time without affecting your family negatively. Wait and listen to Our Lord. Ask him to speak to your heart. Keep in mind that you may not "hear" anything; in fact, most times you will not hear anything. However, the quiet time spent in prayer before Our Lord is very beneficial to our souls. Sometimes our prayer will be without words, but just our thirsty hearts reaching up and seeking out Our Lord. Pope John Paul II spoke about his prayer of no words – being quiet before God and just listening.

Part Two: "To Serve Means to Reign"

1. Serve!

2. Through the Blessed Mother. Pope John Paul II said, "Mary became the first of those who, 'serving Christ also in others, with humility and patience lead her brothers and sisters to that King whom to serve is to reign,' and she fully obtained that 'state of royal freedom' proper to Christ's disciples: to serve means to reign!"

3. a. Serving my husband and children

   b. Doing my household chores

   c. Performing acts of loving service

   Encourage the women to share their ideas and answers.

4. Union with Christ

5. By being obedient to my state in life, which means being a dedicated and loving mother – willing to make the necessary sacrifices for my children

2 – THE GARAGE: A HUSBAND IN THE PICTURE

Part One – Husband and Wife: United in Love

1. Togetherness, holiness, peace, and a loving union are a few attributes. *Encourage the women to come up with more.*

2. Some ways are from Holy Mother Church, her teachings, her documents, through prayer, through associating with like-minded believing Christians.

3. **a.** A husband and wife are united in love through the sacrament and covenant of their marriage and marital vows.

   b. Prayer, praying together, practicing the heroic virtues, and spending time with one another are a few ways to strengthen the bond of love. *Encourage the women to discuss others.*

4. Prayers can be added or incorporated anywhere and any place: at each mealtime, morning and evening, the noontime Angelus, on trips, for special occasions, etc.

Part Two – Differences and Complimentarity

1. Tender, loving, compassionate, strong, nurturing, faithful, intuitive, feminine, etc. *Encourage the women to speak about these attributes, give examples, and add more.*

2. Strong, focused, dedicated, loving, chivalrous, masculine, faithful, etc. *Again, encourage the women to add more and give examples.*

3. Finances, discipline, what to watch on television, goals or projects, etc. *Ask the women to give other examples and perhaps offer solutions to some of these areas of disagreement. This is a good topic to discuss and will be helpful because the women may be able to use some of the advice in their own situations.*

4. Pause to listen, don't interrupt, allow my husband to speak, ask him to allow me to voice my opinion, pray together, pray before and after a major discussion, don't jump to conclusions, give my husband the benefit of the doubt, etc. *Get the women to discuss other ideas.*

5. So that the children see that their parents are together on what they hold to be true regarding rules and values, so that children won't learn to play one parent against the other, for an easier understanding about what is expected of them. *Encourage the women to add their own ideas and discuss.*

6. Prayer is at the top of the list! Practicing the virtues, striving to understand my husband, and realizing that while he does not always think in the

same way as me, he does what he does out of love. When he sees that the garage door is broken, he knows that it needs fixing. He wants his wife to trust him that he is focused on it and that he will fix it. He may not express it eloquently all of the time, just as I won't be able to express myself in a way that is completely understandable to him. Patience with one another is key!

3 – THE BLESSINGS OF LITTLE SOULS

Part One – Open to the Gift of Life: Our "Human and Christian Responsibility"

1. Because we live in a culture that does not necessarily promote life. It promotes personal "freedoms" and confusing messages about "rights" to one's body while leaving out the right of every human being – born and unborn. Catholics know and believe that it can never be right to end an unborn baby's life with abortion or any other way. We also welcome God's gift of life even when there may be defects and illnesses. Every child is unique, unrepeatable, and precious. As Catholic Christians, we will always be a contradiction to the world since the world is not heaven, and it has been referred to as a "valley of tears." We will not live without contradiction until we receive, by God's grace, our eternal life.

Take a few moments to discuss the current affairs of our world and why Christian mothers must be a contraction to the world in so many ways: fashion, values, mothering, etc.

2. Male and female

3. We can read in the Catechism, "So the Church, which 'is on the side of life,' teaches that 'each and every marriage act must remain open to the transmission of life.' This particular doctrine, expounded upon on numerous occasions by the magisterium, is based on the inseparable connection, established by God, which man on his own initiative may not break, between the unitive significance and the procreative significance which are both inherent to the marriage act" (*Humanae Vitae,* 12; cf. Pius XI, *Casti Connubii*).

4. Because artificial means are not in accordance with God's design and in some cases even kills the child. Utilizing the natural rhythm of the human body allows the married couple to be open to life and God's holy will for their marriage.

Part Two: A Special Communion with the Mystery of Life

1. In *Mulieris Dignitatem*, Pope John Paul II expressed, "This unique contact with the new human being developing within her [the mother] gives rise to an attitude towards human beings – not only

towards her own child, but every human being – which profoundly marks the woman's personality. It is commonly thought that *women are more capable than men of paying attention to another person*, and that motherhood develops this predisposition even more." It is really a gift from God. He gives women these motherly hearts in which to love with.

2. A mother's contribution in the early stages of her child's life is "decisive in laying the foundation for a new human personality," Pope John Paul II told us in *Mulieris Dignitatem*. This is because a mother as she raises her child will be a profound influence on him or her, for better or worse. Therefore, it is of the utmost importance for a mother to truly care for her child's needs with much devotion and love.

3. Children play a part in their parent's sanctification because they lead their parents to make the right choices by virtue of the fact that they are dependent on their parents for care and guidance.

Discuss some instances or areas where this may happen. You can use the example of parents who have come back to the Church because they had their baby baptized and decided to embrace the Catholic Church once again. In this case, God used this baby to bring about a change of hearts in the parents. Share some other possible instances of children directing parents.

4. Mothers have a more attached and hands-on job with the children, beginning with the nine months in the womb, the newborn care and feedings, and all of the guiding, training, teaching and everything else that is involved in motherhood.

5. *This is a personal answer. Encourage a discussion, though, if anyone would care to share their answer.*

4 – IN THE HEART OF THE HOME

Part One – Care of the Hearth: Domestic Happiness

1. Because she is the heart of the family. Without her presence at the heart, the family wouldn't function properly. Her gifts are those of the heart, and she is called to give from her heart from her central position in the family.

2. Because he has made her the mother – responsible for mothering and nurturing her children. Our Lord is pleased when a mother devotes herself to the care of her family.

3. Because no one can accurately take the place of the mother in the home. Her children are dependent on the care that she gives to them. They need her presence as she trains them on the road to holiness.

4. A mother should carefully and prayerfully consider any of her desires to work outside the home to discern God's holy will for her, so that she

will not neglect her duties to her children and home life. She should, of course, talk it over with her husband to see what can or should be worked out in this regard.

Part Two – Everyday Holiness: First and Foremost Educator

1. Pope John Paul II also instructed us, "The right and duty of parents to give education is essential, since it is connected with the transmission of human life; it is *original and primary* with regard to the educational role of others, on account of the uniqueness of the loving relationship between parents and children; and it is *irreplaceable and inalienable,* and therefore incapable of being entirely delegated to others or usurped by others."

2. Love

3. *Answers will vary.* Here are some suggestions to make your home a "domestic church":

   a. Teach your family to pray by setting the example of prayer yourself, praying in your children's presence and setting aside times for family prayer at the dinner table and morning and evening.

   b. Observe the Church's liturgical calendar regarding feast days and holy days by celebrating, going to church and participating at holy Mass, making a visit to the Blessed Sacrament, making a special dinner or treat, reading something to the children that is pertinent to the holy day, and teaching the children about the saints.

c. Make a prayer table or "altar" at a central location of your home where you can have a standing crucifix, a statue of the Blessed Mother, a collection of rosary beads, holy water, and the Bible and other spiritual books in a basket or on a bookshelf. A kneeler or pad on the floor in front of the table can be an invitation to kneel and stay a while. You can also hang holy pictures such as the Sacred Heart of Jesus and/or the Immaculate Heart of Mary or icons above the table. All of these things inspire the soul and create a place to pray individually or together.

4. *Answers will vary.* By praying for an increase in faith and specifically asking Our Lord to show you how his hand is within the home. Also, by talking to other Christian mothers who you know are prayerful.

5. By offering your entire day to the Lord the first thing in the morning by praying the words of the Morning Offering or your own version of this prayer, asking Our Lord to use all of your prayers, works, joys, and sufferings of this day in union with all of the Masses said throughout the world today in reparation and for God's grace for sanctification of yourself and your family.

Use examples of a crazy-busy day when all does not go as planned, or the "to do" list didn't get checked off due to various reasons beyond your control. This is a time to acknowledge that God is in control, not us, and that because we have offered our days to him – our lives to him – he blesses it all. We can have faith that he is actually working miracles in human hearts, even though we cannot see the fruits of our labors that day or any day. We need to trust him with a full surrender of our wills.

5 – A VOCATION OF LOVE

Part One – A Love that Compels Us

1. All fear

2. a. Love

   b. *This is a personal answer. Encourage discussion and sharing.*

3. *The answers will vary, as this is a personal answer. Encourage discussion and sharing.*

4. Prayer is an essential ingredient for love to be at the heart of the home. Dedication to motherly duties is paramount. Being faithful to your role as a mother is essential. The practice of virtues – many times heroic virtues – ensures that love is at the root of your mothering in the home. This kind of love requires sacrifice of one's desires and time.

Part Two – A Love that Challenges Us

1. Physically, spiritually, and emotionally. *There can be quite a bit of discussion and sharing here.*

2. *This will be personal for each person.* Yes. The Church speaks about it in encyclicals, letters, and talks, and it continues to research ways to help mothers.

3. a. Physically through pregnancies and childbirth

   b. Putting your own interests and desires on hold while raising your children

   c. Managing with less so you can be more present to your children (not having to work outside the home because you have decided to live with fewer material things, especially those that are not truly necessary).

   d. Another sacrifice may be in dealing with society's attitude that mothers who are not "climbing the corporate ladder" are inferior. *Encourage each participant to share her own personal ideas of sacrifice.*

4. Pray, and ask Our Lord to love through you. Practice the virtues.

6 – PRAYING IN THE DOMESTIC CHURCH

Part One: A Praying Mother – Sanctifying Herself and Her Family

1. Because it is essential to a mother's role within the family. She can't survive properly if she isn't living her prayer life.

2. By offering it all to God, knowing that he knows what is best for the whole family. The sacrifices and sufferings can be powerful prayers for the family when offered to God with love with little or no complaining.

3. *Answers will vary, but encourage the women to share.*

4. a. Personal prayer

   b. Family prayer

   c. Teaching your children to develop their own individual prayer lives

5. *Answers will vary.*

   a. By searching for prayer time actively

   b. By asking your husband to care for the children to allow for some personal prayer time

   c. By accepting what Our Lord gives you with patience, knowing that he is the one who put you in the heart of your home to care for your children

Part Two – A Praying Family: Sanctifying the Ecclesial Community and the World

1. Pope John Paul II told us in *Familiaris Consortio*, "The Christian family too is part of this priestly people which is the Church. By means of the sacrament of marriage, in which it is rooted and from which it draws its nourishment, the Christian family is continuously vivified by the Lord Jesus and called and engaged by him in a dialogue with God through the sacraments, through the offering of one's life, and through prayer."

2. *(Look over quote in answer #1)* Through the sacraments, through the offering of one's life, and through prayer

3. "This is the *priestly role* which the Christian family can and ought to exercise in intimate communion with the whole Church, through the daily realities of married and family life. In this way the Christian family *is called to be sanctified and to sanctify the ecclesial community and the world*" (*Familiaris Consortio*, IV, 55).

4. *Answers may vary.* Here is one quote which refers to the married couple's "priestly" status: "Only by praying together with their children can a father and mother – exercising their royal priesthood – penetrate the innermost depths of their children's hearts and leave an impression that the future events in their lives will not be able to efface" (Pope John Paul II, *Familiaris Consortio*).

5. *Answers will vary.* Here are some suggestions:

   a. By teaching morning prayers, meal prayers, evening prayers

   b. By teaching the children to make good use of every opportunity to pray throughout the day. For instance: thanking God for this day, for the beautiful sunshine or the rain that helps our plants to grow, thanking God for the blessings of the family, and anything else you can imagine.

   c. By teaching your children to offer up their sacrifices and sorrows

   d. By teaching your children to pray for those in need right when the need comes up; for instance, when you hear about someone being sick, or if you see a traffic accident or an ambulance while out with the children, teach them to pause at that very moment and say a prayer.

There are unlimited opportunities for prayer!

6. *Answers will vary.* Some suggestions:

   a. Holy days

   b. Church functions

   c. Mealtimes

   d. Mornings and evenings

   e. The noon Angelus

7 – Selfless Love: The Foot of the Cross

Part One – "A Living Love Hurts"

1. Because to truly love someone, sacrifice is required; otherwise it is not loving with all of your heart

2. *Answers will vary.*

    a. Bringing my children into the world

    b. Giving up my own wants to care for my children

    c. Losing sleep to care for my children, fatigue during the day keeping up with the household, and family demands

    There are many other personal reasons.

3. Not necessarily. The Catechism tells us, "The Beatitudes respond to the natural desire for happiness. This desire is of divine origin: God has placed it in the human heart in order to draw man to the One who alone can fulfill it: 'We all want to live happily; in the whole human race there is no one who does not assent to this proposition, even before it is fully articulated'" (CCC, 1718). So, if we naturally desire happiness, then the question we ask ourselves is: "Is it natural to want to suffer?" While it may not seem natural to want suffering, it is not unnatural to endure suffering for the sake of your loved ones. *Encourage the members to share their ideas.*

4. *This is a personal answer. Open up a discussion and have the women share.*

Levels of personal sacrifice vary with each individual, but see what you can come up with. You may want to give an example or two of your own.

Part Two – A Mother's Beatitudes:
Paradoxical Promises that Sustain Our Hope

1. *This is very personal and may be difficult to answer. Encourage the members to reflect upon this at times throughout the upcoming week and see if they can jot down some other ideas.*

2. *This will also be personal. Encourage each woman to share what they would like.*

3.   a. Their prayer lives

   b. Possibly their values

   c. Their views on suffering and sacrifice for the family

Encourage the women to give their own ideas.

4.   a. By being dedicated to all that Our Lord has for you and your family within his holy will

   b. By surrendering your will to Our Lord's will

   c. By accepting even the suffering he allows you with a hopeful and loving heart

   d. By being a prayerful example to your family by the way you respond to all that is challenging and difficult in your life

e. By teaching your children to offer up their sacrifices and sufferings to God

Encourage the women to share their own thoughts.

8 – An Overflowing Chalice of Love

Part One – Be Kind and Merciful

1. Pope Benedict said, "Once again the Gospel says to us that the love, from the heart of God and operating through the heart of the man, is the force that renews the world." This means that if we allow God to live through us by surrendering our wills to him, we will *become* the "force that renews the world."

Have the women share their thoughts and ask them in what ways might God work through mothers.

2. Pope John Paul II tells us in *Mulieris Dignitatem*, "Woman can only find herself by giving love to others." We mothers *find* ourselves within our service to others – our loving others through our "sincere gift of self." The fruits of a mother's vocation will not only be manifested within her home but also within society, blossoming forth from the sincere gift of herself.

3. We learn from *Familiaris Consortio*, "Thus the Christian family is inspired and guided by the new law of the Spirit and, in intimate communion

with the church, the kingly people; it is called to exercise its 'service' of love towards God and towards its fellow human beings. Just as Christ exercises his royal power by serving us, so also the Christian finds the authentic meaning of his participation in the kingship of his Lord in sharing his spirit and practice of service to man" (FC, 63). A Christian family is a *light* to the world when the family prays and takes Our Lord out into the world through their acts of loving service to others.

Have the women share some ways in which this can be accomplished.

4. Through love, example, and prayer. *Have the group share their insights and thoughts.*

Part Two – Love Knows How to Discover the Face of Christ: Finding God in Each Brother and Sister

1. *Answers will vary.* Serving Our Lord through the Gospel of Matthew 23:31-46 begins in the heart of the home by caring for all of the family's needs. If it is appropriate after all needs are met, a mother can seek ways to serve others outside the doors of the home.

2. a. Prayerfully discuss with your husband

   b. See how it would affect the family and household

   c. If it is appropriate and agreeable with the family, try it out and see how it affects your stamina, your time for household tasks, etc. Of course, we know that when we give love through our active service to others, we strive to give without counting the cost, to allow God to love through us. However, we need to be prudent, as well, and not run ourselves down health-wise – because then we will be of no use to our family which is our first priority. We need to find a proper balance. We can pray about it and listen to what Our Lord is telling us.

3. Through prayer, and also by knowing that the Church teaches us that Our Lord calls us to serve him within every human being ("Just as you did it to one of the least of these who are members of my family, you did it to me)"

Discuss this – have the women share their ideas.

4. We all have a duty to care for one another – first within the family and then to the rest of the world. We can teach our children through our own example, by directly showing them and discussing it with them, by getting them involved in parish ministries, community services, etc.

9 – Evangelizing with the Feminine Genius

Part One – To the Ends of the Earth!

1. *Answers will vary.* Through setting an example of prayer and service to my family. Also, through prayerful discernment about where God is calling me to evangelize out in the world. I need to be mindful that my example within my own home spills out into the world through my children and their connection with those outside, as well as my dealings with the community.

2. Through prayer, through spiritual reading that acknowledges my high calling as a woman, through sharing with other Christian women, as you are doing now through this study

3. *Answers will vary.*

   a. Through your role as first and foremost educator; by teaching prayer and the truth of your Catholic faith to your children and even your spouse in some cases

   b. Through your example of prayer in the household

   c. Through your example of practicing the virtues within your household

Encourage the women to share some of their own ideas.

4. "Animated in its own inner life by missionary zeal, the Church of the home is also called to be a luminous sign of the presence of Christ

and of his love for those who are 'far away,' for families who do not yet believe, and for those Christian families who no longer live in accordance with the faith that they once received. The Christian family is called to enlighten 'by its example and its witness…those who seek the truth,'" we learn from *Familiaris Consortio* (IV, 54) and Second Vatican Ecumenical Council, Dogmatic Constitution on the Church, *Lumen gentium* (35; cf. Decree on the Apostolate of the Laity, *Apostolicam Actuositatem*, 11).

Encourage discussion.

Part Two – Called to Be a Luminous Sign of the Presence of Christ

1. In *Familiaris Consortio* we read, "Just as Christ exercises his royal power by serving us, so also the Christian finds the authentic meaning of his participation in the kingship of the Lord in sharing his spirit and practice of service to man. 'Christ has communicated this power to his disciples that they may be established in royal freedom and that by self-denial and a holy life they might conquer the reign of sin in themselves (cf. Rom. 6:12). Further, he has shared this power so that by serving him in their fellow human beings they might through humility and patience lead their brothers and sisters to that King whom to serve is to reign. For the

Lord wishes to spread his kingdom by means of the laity also, a kingdom of truth and life, a kingdom of holiness and grace, a kingdom of justice, love and peace. In this kingdom, creation itself will be delivered out of its slavery to corruption and into the freedom of the glory of the children of God'" *(FC IV, 63, cf. Rom 8:21)*.

2. *Answers will vary.*

   a. By serving them within a ministry

   b. Through your example

   c. By teaching religious education

   d. By doing the corporal works of mercy:
      - *Feed the hungry*
      - *Give drink to the thirsty*
      - *Clothe the naked*
      - *Shelter the homeless*
      - *Visit the sick*
      - *Visit the imprisoned*
      - *Bury the dead*

   e. By doing the spiritual works of mercy:
      - *Admonish the sinner*
      - *Instruct the ignorant*
      - *Counsel the doubtful*
      - *Comfort the sorrowful*
      - *Bear wrongs patiently*
      - *Forgive all injuries*
      - *Pray for the living and the dead*

3. *Answers will vary.* We read in the Catechism, "Whoever teaches must become 'all things to all men' (1 Cor 9:22), to win everyone to Christ... Above all, teachers must not imagine that a single kind of soul has been entrusted to them, and that consequently it is lawful to teach and form equally all the faithful in true piety with one and the same method! Let them realize that some are in Christ as newborn babes, others as adolescents, and still others as adults in full command of their powers.... Those who are called to the ministry of preaching must suit their words to the maturity and understanding of their hearers, as they hand on the teaching of the mysteries of faith and the rules of moral conduct" (CCC, prologue VI, Roman Catechism, Preface, 11; cf. 1 Cor 9:22; 1 Pet 2:2). *Read this quote to the members and invite them to share their ideas of what it is to become "all things to all men."*

4. *Answers will vary.*

   a. By *thirsting* for Christ

   b. By *listening* to Christ

   c. By giving up the clutter in your mind and your heart to be filled with the *living water*

   d. By becoming a missionary, as the woman at the well did, by running out to tell the others about Jesus and his *living water*

Ask the women to share their personal responses to this question.

ACKNOWLEDGEMENTS

For all of the mothers in my life:
Thank you for mothering me!

To my mother, Alexandra Mary Uzwiak Cooper:
in loving memory and gratitude for bringing me into this world against
her doctor's orders, and for teaching me the necessity of prayer and
how to give without ever counting the cost.

In loving memory and gratitude to my grandmother:
Alexandra Theresa Karasiewicz Uzwiak for her inexhaustible love,
guidance, and inspiration.

To my godmother: Aunt Bertha Uzwiak Barosky, in gratitude for her
loving prayers and guidance throughout my life.

In loving memory of Blessed Teresa of Calcutta,
with gratitude for her inspiration. Her consistent encouragement to me
to continue to write to help others, especially mothers,
has certainly given me much courage and motivation.
Her faith in me, her prayers, and her love for me has left a
permanent imprint on my heart.

To dear Mother Mary, our Blessed Mother,
who has always watched over me during my lifetime, my gratitude
for her motherly influence, love, and protection that has
forever been my saving grace.

To all others I hold dear:

In loving memory of my father, Eugene Joseph Cooper, who along with
my mother brought me into this world – with gratitude for his love and support, and for
working so hard to care for our large family.

To my brothers and sisters: Alice Jean, Gene, Gary, Barbara, Tim, Michael, and David.
Thank you for your love.

To my godfather, Uncle Alfred Uzwiak, for his love and concern throughout my life.

With grateful thanks to my dear friend and spiritual guide, the late
Father William C. Smith, for his cherished friendship, love, and blessed guidance.

With grateful thanks to my friend, spiritual guide, and my daughter's godfather,
the late Father John A. Hardon, SJ, for all of his marvelous wisdom and
continued prayers and guidance from heaven.

To my dear friends, Father Peter Towsley and Father James Farfaglia, for their treasured
friendship and their many prayers for me and my family. I am most grateful.

To my husband, David, my partner and best friend. Thank you for believing
in me and loving me. I love you.

In loving memory of dear Pope John Paul the Great, with gratitude for his inexhaustible
wisdom and blessings in the profound and selfless love of his shepherding, which I was
able to benefit from throughout a good part of my lifetime.

I would also like to thank Claudia Volkman of Circle Press who has been very
wonderful to work with on this project. My thanks to the whole team for their support
and efforts to enable this study for mothers to reach mothers and women everywhere.
I'd also like to thank Jim O'Day for his friendship and support of my work,
and for introducing me to Claudia.

Lastly, with heartfelt gratefulness, I want to thank my readers for their friendship
and prayers for my journey. I hope they will feel assured of my continued prayers for all
of them in their journeys on the road that leads to life!

ABOUT THE AUTHOR

Donna-Marie Cooper O'Boyle speaks to a mother's heart about the blessings, grace, and lessons learned throughout her spiritual journey during motherhood. She has received awards for her work and is the author of the best-selling books, *Catholic Prayer Book for Mothers* (Our Sunday Visitor, 2005), *The Heart of Motherhood, Finding Holiness in the Catholic Home* (Crossroad, 2006), *Prayerfully Expecting: A Nine Month Novena for Mothers-to-Be* (Crossroad, 2007), which includes a Foreword by Blessed Teresa of Calcutta, and *Catholic Saints Prayer Book* (Our Sunday Visitor, 2008). Donna-Marie's books were endorsed by Blessed Teresa of Calcutta and given the prestigious honor of an apostolic blessing from Pope John Paul II.

Donna-Marie grew up in a large, close-knit Catholic family, admiring God's majesty in the beauty of nature surrounding her, as she sought out holiness and searched for a deeper meaning in life.

Embracing family life, she became a wife and mother of five. She also served as a prioress and mistress of novices for the Third Order of St. Dominic branch, which she helped to start. She founded a branch of the Lay Missionaries of Charity, taught religious education for over twenty years, and was a Eucharistic minister to the sick. Donna-Marie founded the Angels of Mercy, the Marian Mothers, Apostles of the Blessed Sacrament, and Friends of Veronica, an outreach to senior citizens and the lonely in answer to the call in the Gospel of Matthew 25:31-46. Donna-Marie is a Lay Missionary of Charity.

In God's divine providence, Donna-Marie met Blessed Teresa of Calcutta and remained in contact with her for a decade, meeting and corresponding with her. Donna-Marie is passionate about sharing with other mothers her inspiration and "heart-to-hearts" she had with her beloved friend, Blessed Teresa, as well as her own personal experiences and insights to encourage mothers and help them to see the sublimity in their vocation of motherhood.

The Holy See through The Pontifical Council for the Laity invited Donna-Marie to Rome in February 2008 to participate in an international congress, "Woman and Man: The 'Humanum' in Its Entirety" on the occasion of the twentieth anniversary of *Mulieris Dignitatem*: On the Dignity and Vocation of Women.

Donna-Marie's work can be seen in several Catholic magazines, newspapers, and on the Internet at several Web sites and columns. She has been profiled on many television shows, including *Faith & Culture* on EWTN as well as EWTN's *Bookmark* with Doug Keck. Donna-Marie can be heard discussing parenting issues with Teresa Tomeo on a regular radio show, "Mom's Corner" on "Catholic Connection," Ave Maria Radio. She lectures on topics relating to Catholic and Christian women and families and can be reached at her Web site, http://www.donnacooperoboyle.com. She provides daily inspiration at her blogs: "Embracing Motherhood" at http://www.donnamarieembracingmotherhood.blogspot.com, "Daily Donna-Marie" at http://www.donnamariecooperoboyle.blogspot.com, and "Moments of Inspiration with Your Favorite Saints" at http://www.momentsofinspirationsaints.blogspot.com.

She welcomes your visits and hopes that you know,

"We are all on this journey together!"